EUROPEAN FIREARMS

VICTORIA AND ALBERT MUSEUM

EUROPEAN FIREARMS

BY J. F. HAYWARD

LONDON: HER MAJESTY'S STATIONERY OFFICE

1955

First published . . February, 1955.
Sold at the Victoria and Albert Museum,
South Kensington, and by Her Majesty's
Stationery Office at the addresses given
on page 3 of cover. Crown copyright
reserved. Printed in Great Britain by
W. S. Cowell Ltd, at the Butter Market,
Ipswich.

FOREWORD

THE INTENTION of this work is to provide a guide to the Museum Collection of firearms, not to offer a general history of the subject. The numerous historical and technical problems which are likely to be encountered by the student of the subject are therefore only discussed in so far as they arise in connection with objects in the Museum collection. This collection, having come to the Museum almost entirely through gift or bequest, have not been assembled according to any consistent policy of acquisition and there are numerous gaps in relation both to technical development and decorative design. Recent acquisitions have all been purchased out of a fund bequeathed by Major V. A. Farquharson, F.S.A. who also gave his collection to the Museum. The name of this benefactor will be encountered frequently in the catalogue of selected pieces which forms the main body of this guide, and even more so in the Gallery where the collection is exhibited. The examples described and illustrated in the catalogue have been selected from the main collection on grounds, firstly, of artistic merit and, secondly, of technical or historical interest. The fact that any particular type of mechanism or ornament is not represented in the illustrations does not necessarily imply that there is no example in the Museum.

This handbook has been written by Mr. J. F. Hayward, Assistant Keeper in the Department of Metalwork. Acknowledgements are due to Dr. Torsten Lenk, director of the Royal Armoury, Stockholm, and Dr. Arne Hoff, Curator of Firearms at the Arsenal Museum, Copenhagen, for reading the text and for making many valuable suggestions and corrections.

November 1954

LEIGH ASHTON,
Director

EUROPEAN FIREARMS

THE HISTORY of firearms has in recent years been the subject of a great volume of research, particularly as regards technical development. Though the main course of their evolution is now established, there are still many gaps in our knowledge, mostly relating to the origins of certain lock mechanisms and certain types of ornament. A firearm is a complex piece of mechanism in the production of which workmen of several different crafts must combine. The manufacture of barrel, lock, stock and mounts each requires different equipment and different types of skill and throughout the centuries it has only been the most prosperous gunmakers who have been able to assemble all the workmen required for these various processes under one roof. In the sixteenth and seventeenth centuries not only would it be exceptional for a gunmaker to carry out all the processes of manufacture in his own workshop, but the craftsmen who made firearms belonged to different guilds, the barrel-smith to the Blacksmiths' Guild, the lock-makers to the Locksmiths' Guild, the stock-makers to the Joiners' Guild and the makers of silver mounts to the Goldsmiths' Guild. The situation varied very much from town to town and country to country, but even in Augsburg and Nürnberg, where gunmaking developed on a large scale as early as the middle of the sixteenth century, the gunmakers did not form their own guild until the seventeenth century. The same is true of Munich and Vienna. In London the Gunmakers' Company was first established in 1637, the gunmakers having previously belonged to the Armourers' or Blacksmiths' Company.

The division of labour between different workshops was particularly marked in Germany in the sixteenth and seventeenth centuries, and in Northern Italy in the seventeenth century. The eventual result of this division was that the gunmaker whose signature appeared on the lock or barrel was no more than a gun finisher who assembled parts which he had purchased wholesale from specialist workshops. If one examines a typical German wheel-lock rifle of the seventeenth century, it is likely that the signatures of three or even four different craftsmen will be found on it, that of the barrel-smith on the breech of the barrel, that of the locksmith on the lock, that of the gunstocker engraved or stamped behind the tang of the barrel, and, in the case of some finely-decorated arms, that of the chiseller (Eisenschneider) concealed within the decoration of the lock, barrel or mounts. Specialization within the workshops on the manufacture of locks or barrels was paralleled by the establishment of specialized industries in certain towns. Suhl in Germany, Eibar and Madrid in Spain, Gardone near Brescia in Italy specialized in the production of barrels. Wheel-locks were, during the sixteenth century, manufactured on a large scale for export in Augsburg and Nürnberg. When a weapon of the highest quality was ordered from a provincial German gunsmith in the early seventeenth century, it is quite likely that he would have obtained the barrel from Suhl, a fine quality lock from Augsburg, and then have sent the iron parts to Munich for decoration and gilding by the celebrated school of iron-chisellers that worked for the Bavarian Court. Finally, he would probably have had the stock made by a local craftsman.

Some of the centres of gunmaking, such as Brescia, Ripoll in Catalonia or Eger in Bohemia, had their own clearly-defined style of ornament and techniques of manufacture to which the local craftsmen remained constant for long periods. Other centres such as the German cities of Augsburg or Nürnberg were more cosmopolitan in character, and though they might have their own local conventions, they were capable of producing weapons in whatever style their patrons might require. No. 15 (Plate IV), a pistol made in Nürnberg in 1593, is for instance, equipped with a lock with independently fixed main-spring, a type otherwise confined to the gunmakers of France and the territories on the northern borders of France. Another cause of confusion in recognizing the place of manu-facture of a particular piece is the fact that gunsmiths, after serving as apprentices in a large centre such as Augsburg, Liége or Paris, would move to some smaller town in their own country or even emigrate abroad, where, however, they might continue to work in the manner they had learnt during their apprenticeship. Thus we find the Augsburg gun-makers, who were brought by Charles V to work at his court in Madrid, producing fire-arms there which give no hint of their actual place of manufacture. The local tradition invariably reasserted itself in the long run and the arrival of such immigrants made no permanent impression upon the national school of gunmaking where such existed. The large scale emigration of French Huguenot gunmakers after the Revocation of the Edict of Nantes in 1685 led, for instance, to the presence of highly-skilled Parisian gunmakers in London and other European capitals, but did not result in the lasting adoption of Parisian standards of form and decoration. Some of the firearms made in London by the Parisian gunsmith Monlong were as fine as any made in Paris at the time, but to judge by a pistol in the Museum (No. 62, Plate XXIV) he seems eventually to have adopted the less exacting English standards, presumably owing to the lack of a sufficient number of wealthy patrons, or the difficulty of finding sufficiently skilled workmen.

Another exception to local or national practice is found sometimes in the work of the Court gunmakers. In the sixteenth and seventeenth centuries the more powerful European princes maintained one or more gunmakers amongst the artists and craftsmen attached to their court. The Museum collections include a number of firearms signed by court gun-makers (Nos. 73, 75, 77 and 79 in the catalogue). The large financial resources of some princes enabled them to maintain foreign craftsmen at their courts, sometimes practising a style which was quite exotic. As an example, one may quote the weapons made in a hybrid Italo-German style by the gunmakers to the Dukes of Saxe-Weimar which are not, however, represented in the Museum. The Prague workshop of the Emperor Rudolph II also turned out some remarkable firearms, including the wheel-lock rifle now in the Kunsthistorisches Museum, Vienna, with silver stock decorated in translucent enamel by David Altenstetter, the barrel and mounts decorated by Daniel Sadeler.

The mere fact that a firearm bears a Nürnberg town mark (Beschauzeichen) on the barrel, or the signature of a Liége maker on the lock does not tell the whole story of its origin, and before attributing it to a particular source it is necessary to consider the form, workmanship and ornament of the other parts which constitute it. The following prin-ciples can be regarded as generally valid.

With the exception of the earliest period of gunmaking, barrel making was quite a separate trade. Even if the name on the lock is repeated on the barrel, this probably means no more than that the lock-maker has finished the barrel. The gunmaker proper was usually the lock-maker who assembled barrel, stock and mounts, finished them and fitted them with a lock. Normally the ornamentation of the stock with carving or bone inlay and of the lock and mounts with damascening would have been carried out in the gunmaker's own workshop, but where an exceptionally richly ornamented piece was required, such as the air gun (No. 78, Plate XXXI), the assistance of professional goldsmiths or engravers was obtained. It was not till about the middle of the seventeenth century that it became usual for the gunmaker to sign his name in full. Earlier, we find a lock-smith's stamp and a barrel-smith's stamp, and, in the case of German firearms, the initials of the stocker as well. In the second half of the seventeenth century and subsequently, we usually find the maker's name on the lock, sometimes repeated on the barrel. In the case of Brescian firearms, the lock and barrel were signed separately, but, as a rule, from about 1680 one name only appears on a European firearm, the barrel-smith's mark being struck on the underside of the barrel where it was concealed by the stock. The main exception to this rule is encountered in the practice of the English barrel-smiths of stamping their barrels on the upper side. The English Gunmakers' Company, to which all barrels mounted up by the London gunmakers had to be submitted for proof, also applied their marks on the left-hand upper side of the breech. It will frequently be found that the initials of the barrel-smith do not correspond with the name on the lock.

The ornament on firearms has for the most part been drawn from printed pattern books. The main exceptions to this generalization are to be found in certain local schools of gun-making which were able to draw on an indigenous style of ornament. Besides the Scottish gunmakers, who continued to employ Celtic ornament until late in the eighteenth century, the schools of Brescia, Ripoll and Naples, may be cited. As soon as it became the practice to apply elaborate ornament to a firearm, the gunmaker found it necessary to look beyond his own resources or those of his workshop in order to find patterns appropriate for decorating his productions.

Throughout the sixteenth century a constant supply of ornamental designs was issued by the engravers of Nürnberg and Augsburg, such as Peter Flötner, Virgil Solis and, later, Jost Amman. During the sixteenth century, these same cities of Augsburg and Nürnberg were also the largest manufacturing centres of firearms, and, as might be expected, the gunmakers made use of the designs produced by their fellow citizens. The majority of the engraved ornament on sixteenth-century German firearms can be traced back to the œuvre of one or other of quite a small group of engravers, working in either Augsburg or Nürnberg. Towards the end of the sixteenth century, the designs of the French artist, Etienne Delaune, were much used, particularly by the Munich school, but it should be remembered that this master spent some years in Germany and that many of his designs were published there.

While the sixteenth-century engravers produced designs for cups, bowls and other examples of goldsmith's work, they did not publish designs specifically intended for application to the peculiar form and shape of a match-lock or wheel-lock firearm. It was, therefore, necessary for the gunsmith to adapt the designs he found in the pattern-book to the shape of the lock, stock and other parts of the firearm. This work was doubtless as a rule carried out in the gunmaker's own workshop, but it is probable that where a fire-arm of unusual splendour of ornament was required, the assistance of a professional engraver may have been called in. The Museum Collection includes a series of sixty water-colour drawings of designs for the decoration of various parts of wheel-lock gun-stocks derived from the pattern books of Virgil Solis, Jost Amman and Paul Flindt, all artists of Nürnberg. Some of these (Nos. 9–12, 13, 14) are shown in Plates I and V; they illustrate the intermediate stage that was necessary between the printed pattern-book and the decorated firearm.

As the demand for decorated firearms became greater, the engravers found it worth while to issue books of ornament specially designed so that the ornament could be copied directly by gunmakers without the necessity for adaption. The earliest of these is a series of engravings of wheel-locks of French type, dating from the latter part of the sixteenth century and attributed to a follower of the French engraver, Androuet Ducerceau. There-after, an unbroken series of designs for firearms were produced by Parisian artists, covering practically every variation of fashion in ornament from the beginning of the seventeenth century up till the early nineteenth century. It is a peculiar fact that almost all the books of designs for gun ornament were the work of engravers working in Paris. Pirated editions appeared in Holland and Germany under other names but the credit for all origi-nal work of this nature must go to France. The French designs of the second half of the seventeenth century evidently had a wide circulation outside the borders of France, and we find firearms made after the French pattern books by gunmakers in practically every European country. The most influential works were probably the two books issued by the two Simonins (Nos. 57, 58, Plate XXIII), in 1685 and 1693 respectively which appeared without acknowledgement later in two German editions and a Dutch edition. The Museum collection of engraved ornament in the Department of Engravings, Illustration and Design, includes all the important pattern books of firearms.

It was the practice in the gunmakers' workshops of the seventeenth and eighteenth centuries for the engraver to take a pull of the designs he executed on the metal parts of firearms. These were retained in the workshop, presumably as a record to prevent repeti-tion of the same design. Such working pulls have survived in considerable numbers (Nos. 37–43, Plates XV, XVI) and are well represented in the Department of Engraving, Illu-stration and Design, where there are examples dating from the mid-seventeenth up to the nineteenth century. As the pull was taken directly from the engraved lock-plate or mount, the design and signature, if any, appears in reverse. It is an interesting fact that amongst a group of these pulls from lock-plates engraved apparently by the same hand, a number of different gunmaker's signatures may be found. This would appear to indicate that, at any rate in the seventeenth century, one engraver decorated lock-plates and mounts for a number of the gunmakers working in his town. A similar conclusion may be drawn from the book of designs engraved by Jacquinet for 'Thuraine et le Hollandios,

4

Arquebuziers Ordinaires de Sa Majesté' published in Paris in 1660 (No. 44, Plate XVII). It is evident that Jacquinet was a gun decorator by profession and in this work he shows not only locks engraved by him for 'Thuraine et le Hollandois' but also others executed for a number of other Parisian masters.

The Museum collections of firearms have been assembled primarily with the intention of illustrating progress of design and ornament. They consist almost exclusively of pieces made for wealthy clients, and the plain military arms, which have always constituted the bulk of firearms production, are not represented. The collection begins at about 1540, a comparatively advanced date in the evolution of firearms. By this date both match-lock and wheel-lock mechanisms were in use. By the middle of the sixteenth century, the wheel-lock had already passed through nearly half a century of development and had reached the form which it was substantially to retain for the next 150 years. It was a German invention and for the greater part of the sixteenth century the German cities of Nürnberg, Augsburg, Munich, Dresden and possibly Brunswick had almost a monopoly of its manufacture. Nearly all the surviving sixteenth-century wheel-lock firearms are of German manufacture or were produced within the German sphere of influence, that is, in the Dutch-speaking Netherlands or, towards the end of the century, in Denmark. The wheel-locks made in Amsterdam or in Copenhagen follow closely the German pattern, so much so that in the earlier days it is difficult to be certain whether a lock was made by an immigrant German craftsman or whether it was imported ready-made for mounting on a locally-made stock and barrel.

Traditionally, the invention of the wheel-lock mechanism has been attributed to a certain Johann Kiefuss of Nürnberg in the year 1517. It is not likely to have been invented outright and it has been suggested that it may have evolved from the spring-driven tinder-lighters which were in use at the time. The traditional account must be approximately correct for there seems no reason to doubt that the wheel-lock originated in South Germany, in Augsburg or Nürnberg, at the beginning of the sixteenth century.

Though there are a few wheel-lock firearms in existence which have tentatively been dated even earlier, those made for the Emperor Charles V which are preserved in the Real Armeria at Madrid constitute our most important evidence as to the beginning of the wheel-lock. As there are drawings of many of them in the *Inventario Illuminado* of the Armoury of Charles V and as some of them are dated and bear the mark of one or other of the two Augsburg gunsmiths, Peter and Simon Markwart, who were brought to Madrid by order of the Emperor, they provide a reliable corpus of evidence.

The Charles V wheel-lock firearms consist of short carbines, evidently intended to be carried in holsters attached to the saddle, and pistols, both single and double barrelled. The carbines show already the *deutsche Kolbe* form, that is, the butts are straight sided, of angular section and are not intended to be set against the shoulder; the pistols have straight butts, continuing in the axis of the barrel. They bear dates between 1530 and 1547 and, though not the earliest wheel-locks in existence, they well illustrate the forms in use during the second quarter of the sixteenth century. While all have the same general type of lock, three different ways of attaching the cock spring are represented, a crescent-shaped spring

5

placed around the lower half of the wheel with an arm extending across to the foot of the cock, a V-shaped spring placed on the inner side of the lock-plate and a V-shaped spring placed under the arm of the cock. An example of the first type is illustrated in Plate I (No. 1), of the third in Plate II (No. 6); no example of the second is illustrated here, but the type may be seen on the iron-stocked pistol (M.628–1927), which is dated 1579.

Amongst Charles V's firearms, the first type appears on a piece dated 1534, the second on one dated 1537, and the third on one dated 1531. It is probable that these types originated in different German cities, type 1 being associated with Nürnberg, and type 3 more with Augsburg, but we have no means of identifying their sources with certainty. In any case the various forms would doubtless have been adopted with little delay by gunsmiths working in other German cities. Of the three types, it was the third that became the standard form. The first barely survived into the second half of the sixteenth century, the second dropped out towards the end of the sixteenth century, but is found in a modified form on some locks of the second half of the seventeenth century.

Of the third type there were two forms. In one, the arms of the V spring were of equal length, in the other, the lower arm was considerably shorter than the upper (No. 29, Plate XII). The form with arms of unequal length may have originated in Augsburg; it is certainly found on a considerable number of firearms bearing the Augsburg *Beschauzeichen* (town mark). Whatever its origin, it was soon copied elsewhere.

The wheel-lock firearms dating from about the middle of the sixteenth century or earlier show certain common features. These include, firstly, the long drawn out shape of the lock-plate and, secondly, the fact that the arm of the cock is perfectly straight, without the angle which developed about the middle of the century. The form of the stocks also assists in identifying early wheel-lock firearms. In the case of the sixteenth-century arquebus, the sides of the butt are almost parallel (No. 5, Plate II); early in the seventeenth century the stock widens out slightly towards the butt-plate and a wide flange is formed below the cheek-piece (Plate VI). In the case of pistols, it is probable that the form of the butt was derived from the handle of the mace or war hammer. Some of the pistols of Charles V have butts in line with the barrel, like a mace handle. This form dates from about 1530–40, and as the century advanced, the angle between the axis of the barrel and the butt became less obtuse, until by the 1590's we find sharp angles, as on the Nürnberg pistol (No. 15, Plate IV) which is dated 1593. The fact that the angle between stock and barrel is slight is not however decisive proof of early date, for the straight butt returned to favour during the first half of the seventeenth century (No. 22, Plate VIII). Towards the end of the sixteenth century we find two types of pistol ordered for the Bodyguard of the Elector of Saxony, the first with straight or nearly straight stocks, the second (e.g. M64–1950) with butts set at an angle.

During the second half of the sixteenth century, two forms of lock-plates are found on German wheel-lock firearms. The earlier of these has a fairly straight lower profile, apart from a marked upward curve in front of the wheel (No. 19, Plate VII), the other has a lock-plate of approximately lozenge shape (No. 29, Plate XII). Another interesting feature of this second type, which possibly originated in Augsburg, is the presence of an indentation cut in the lower edge of the lock-plate below the cock-spring. On the early pieces, dating from the mid-sixteenth century this indentation is long, but it becomes gradually shorter until by the seventeenth century it is quite short (No. 29, Plate XII). As Dr. Lenk has shown, it is from this S. German lock form with indentation in the lower edge that the Italian wheel-lock was developed. Certain further characteristics can be recognized, in the first type the lower jaw of the cock forms one piece with the arm of the cock, while the upper jaw is retained by the cock screw, in the second the position is reversed, the upper jaw forming one piece with the arm while the lower jaw is free. The modelling of the cock was also affected, thus with the first type the cock face is usually flat, with the second it is usually rounded. This distinction has a certain geographical validity, though not in Central Germany where both types were used equally. In Western Germany, Italy and France, the type with fixed upper jaw was with few exceptions normal. One exception may be seen in the French wheel-lock (No. 26, Plate X).

Most of the pistols of Charles V are surprisingly plain, but even during the first half of the sixteenth century it became usual to decorate firearms made for rich patrons in a most elaborate manner. In Germany the stocks were decorated with marquetry or inlay of engraved stag-horn and mother of pearl, while the metal parts were damascened with gold and silver. There are no early examples of the richest ornament in the Museum, but the detached locks, No. M.493–1927 and No. 18 (Plate XVII) show the style in the last quarter of the sixteenth century while the pistol (No. 23, Plate VIII) shows it in the early years of the seventeenth century.

The earlier German arquebus stocks provided only restricted space for inlay work, but as the butt widened out towards the end of the century, the opportunity for the inlay worker was greatly increased. Fine quality inlay can be seen on the stocks illustrated in Plates VI to IX, but there is a more important display of this German inlay and marquetry work amongst the wheel-lock firearms in the Wallace Collection. In examining the inlay work and engraving it is necessary to remember that once a pattern book was acquired by a gunstocker it continued in use in his workshop over a very long period. We find therefore the designs of the sixteenth-century artists, Virgil Solis, Adriaen Collaert and Jost Amman being applied to wheel-lock gunstocks in Germany in the mid-seventeenth century and even later.

The work of the steel chisellers to the Bavarian Court, who were active during approximately the hundred years from about 1580 to 1680, is the best known of the German schools of fine steel working. These artists were primarily decorators and chiselled not only firearms but sword hilts, knife hafts, purse mounts, boxes and, in fact, whatever they were commissioned to do. Their work as applied to firearms is not very well represented in the Museum. There is a superbly chiselled lock (No. 29, Plate XII) for a wheel-lock pistol dating from the beginning of the seventeenth century, but the magnificence of their richest productions can best be seen in the Wallace Collection in London. The work of these Munich masters, the brothers Emanuel and Daniel Sadeler and their successor, Caspar Spät, probably represents the highest level ever achieved in the decorative treatment of arms, but there were certainly other masters, hitherto anonymous, who may in the future be recognized as almost approaching them. The Electors of Saxony, the Dukes of Brunswick and, finally, the Hapsburg Emperors all had their own court gunsmiths who doubtless sought to equal the achievement of the Sadelers. The pair of pistols for which a design exists in the Museum (No. 7, Plate III) must, if they were ever executed, have been of a magnificence comparable with that of the weapons made for the Dukes of Bavaria.

The shape of the German arquebus stock is always a puzzle to the uninformed. It was not intended to be discharged from the shoulder, nor could it be held in such a way as to bring it to the shoulder. It was apparently held against the cheek, clear of the shoulder, and the recoil was taken with the arms. The stag-horn inlay on the stocks often shows a hunting scene with a hunter discharging his wheel-lock rifle in this way. The considerable weight of the barrel and stock of the typical German wheel-lock was sufficient to absorb much of the force of the recoil. Geographically this type of stock was confined to the German-speaking regions and Scandinavia. Elsewhere a butt of rounded form was used, probably developed from the hooked butt of the match-lock musket. The original form can be seen in No. 2, Plate II, and its more developed form in the heavy French musket, formerly in the personal armoury of King Louis XIII (No. 27, Plate X).

The German gunsmiths of the sixteenth century devoted a great deal of ingenuity to improving the wheel-lock firearm. Not merely was rifling introduced, but double and triple barrelled weapons, breech-loading guns and the super-imposed load system were developed. The Museum collections include an arquebus with two touch holes for super-imposed charges dated 1581 (No. 5, Plate II), a double-barrelled wheel-lock petronel of about 1600 (No. 16, Plate XV), a wheel-lock rifle of 1605 (No. 20, Plate VI), a wheel-lock breech-loading pistol of about 1600; the system of this last is the same as that of the two arquebuses of Henry VIII in the Tower of London, which cannot be later than about 1540. Finally there is a wheel-lock, with gear-wheels so that the wheel is spanned automatically when the cock is drawn back, of about 1550 (No. 1, Plate I). All these pieces are of German origin.

The above remarks have been mainly confined to German wheel-lock firearms. Match-lock firearms had been manufactured in France, Holland and Italy during the sixteenth century in considerable numbers. Most of these were plain military arms, the rich ornament being reserved for wheel-lock sporting arms. However, a number of very finely inlaid German match-lock muskets exist and a French example is illustrated (No. 2, Plate II). It will be seen that the ornament, of horn, partly stained green, and mother of pearl, does not differ in general character from that in use in Germany at the same time. Subsequently, towards the end of the sixteenth century, the French gunstockers developed a style entirely of their own which showed no trace of German influence.

Production of wheel-lock firearms probably began in Holland during the third quarter of the sixteenth century and in Italy perhaps slightly later. While the Dutch and the Italians copied the German form of lock, the French gunsmiths developed their own form of wheel-lock which differed constructionally from the German system. Apart from a difference in the profile of the lock-plate the French lock-plate, being of smaller

8

dimensions (No. 17, Plate I), the main distinctions were, firstly, that the mainspring was not attached to the lock-plate but was fixed independently by a pin passing through the stock, and secondly that the spindle on which the wheel rotated passed right through the stock and keyed into a recess cut in a steel side-plate inset in the stock on the opposite side to the lock. In general, it may be taken as a rule that the presence of this type of mechanism marks a firearm as French, but the pistol No. 15, Plate IV, which is of Nürnberg manufacture, presents an exception. The French double-barrelled pistol (No. 26, Plate X) is, conversely, equipped with the German type of lock—for the good reason that it would be very difficult to accommodate two separately attached mainsprings within the narrow compass of a pistol stock.

No reference has yet been made to the snaphaunce lock which was widely used in Europe during the seventeenth century. Its source is uncertain, but the earliest known examples are of Scandinavian origin and date from the middle of the sixteenth century. The lock was also produced in Germany during the sixteenth century, and there is a Nürnberg marked snaphaunce lock of the second half of the sixteenth century in the Tower of London. There is a reference to a payment by the Stuttgart Court for a number of Landsknecht muskets with snaphaunces in the year 1584, followed subsequently by further payments. Towards the end of the sixteenth century, the snaphaunce spread to Holland and, about the turn of the century, to Scotland. It was, however, mainly employed for plain military weapons in the sixteenth century, and most of these have now perished. There exists a group of early seventeenth-century muskets with either match-lock or snaphaunce ignition, the stocks of which are profusely inlaid with engraved mother of pearl and with brass wire, in a manner similar to but coarser than the contemporary French work. Some of these muskets have the Amsterdam town mark on either lock or barrel. There is a fork for a musket of this type in the Museum (2190–1855). During the seventeenth century, the snaphaunce system found little demand except for military purposes outside Scandinavia, Scotland and North Italy.

By the latter part of the sixteenth century, the gunmakers of Germany may be divided geographically into two main groups, those of the south and east, centred in Augsburg, Nürnberg, Munich and Dresden, and those of the west in the Aachen-Köln area. While the gunsmiths of the south-eastern area during the first half of the seventeenth century followed on in the sixteenth century tradition, in the west a new grouping covering the Rhineland, Switzerland, Holland and Alsace-Lorraine becomes increasingly marked. The firearms made in this region represent a style half-way between the South German and the French manner. Wheel-lock pistols of this group are well represented in the Museum collection. The earliest is probably the Alsace-Lorraine type pistol, the stock of which is inlaid with rather coarsely-engraved mother of pearl and horn, interspersed with brass wire. This type of pistol is found in association with both the German and the French wheel-lock construction (No. 28, Plate VIII). The ornament is derived from French or Dutch rather than the German prototypes. The German influenced style can be seen in the pair of unsigned pistols (No. 31, Plate XI) with silver inlaid stocks. The designs engraved on the silver are copied from the engravings of Michel Le Blon, a German-born

9

artist of Flemish extraction who was working in the Dutch city of Amsterdam. The Dutch type is represented by the plain pair of military pistols (M.632, 632a–1927). Finally the Swiss version is represented by No. 30 (Plate XI), a pair of wheel-lock pistols with brass lock-plates and barrels, some of the ornamental details of which have also been taken from designs by Michel Le Blon. The Thirty Years War in Europe kept the gunsmiths busy and this area, which was outside the main area of operations, must have supplied large quantities of arms. In comparison with the French firearms, the pieces from the territories around the French northern borders are coarse and lacking in grace.

During the first quarter of the seventeenth century, the pistol lock was made considerably lighter by a reduction in size of the lock-plate. At the same time the heavy wheel-cover which was secured to the lock-plate by two screws, one on each side, was replaced by a light hook, usually set on the left-hand side of the wheel. The wheel-cover continued to be applied to the locks made for rifles and arquebuses, and was often attractively decorated. In the Museum there are examples in pierced and engraved steel, pierced, engraved and gilt brass and in cast brass. Examples of silver and of enamelled copper are also known.

If the sixteenth century was dominated by the German gunsmiths, the seventeenth century saw the emergence of Paris as the home of the pre-eminent gunmakers of Europe. The French proved not only to be leaders in technical development but also in design, and we find the most remarkable contrast between the clumsy German ball-butted 'Puffer' (No. 8, Plate IV) and the elegant French wheel-lock pistols of the first half of the seventeenth century, the best of which are unfortunately not represented in the Museum. Some of the French wheel-lock pistols are so finely and delicately worked that they look quite unsuited to contain the discharge of so violent a medium as gunpowder. It was in the combination of technical efficiency with refinement of form that the French genius asserted itself. It is, moreover, to a craftsman at the French Court, Marin le Bourgeois, that the credit of developing the true flint-lock mechanism in the first decade or so of the seventeenth century should probably be given.

The French gunmakers were doubtless encouraged by the fact that King Louis XIII was from an early age interested in firearms. The diary of his medical attendant Jehan Heroard, mentions that in 1611, when he was ten years old, he already owned seven arquebuses. By 1614 he had a collection of fifty and he was constantly purchasing more. One of his favourite occupations was to dismount and clean his firearms himself. His personal 'Cabinet d'Armes', containing hundreds of firearms, seems to have survived intact until the French Revolution. In 1673 his collection was inventoried by order of Louis XIV; and, as the inventory numbers were stamped on the stocks of each of the firearms, it is possible to identify the firearms which originally belonged to him. Eight of these are in the Museum collection and a number are in the Tower of London and the Wallace Collection. The exact fate of the Cabinet d'Armes after the Revolution is uncertain. It seems likely that at an earlier date the more decorative pieces had been separated from the plain arms of military type, of which Louis XIII had a number. The latter were placed in the Paris Arsenal where they remained until the occupation of Paris by the victorious allied troops after the Battle of Waterloo. Both the Prussians and the British removed quantities of firearms from the Arsenal as captured warlike stores. The trophies taken by the British, which included many firearms from the former royal 'Cabinet d'Armes' were originally placed in the Royal Artillery Museum at Woolwich, whence in recent years they have been transferred, in part to the Tower of London, and in part to the Victoria and Albert Museum.

The guns from Louis XIII's collection in this Museum show his interest in all kinds of firearms. They include a wheel-lock arquebus (No. 27, Plate X), a wheel-lock double-barrelled pistol (No. 26, Plate X) and a series of three muskets, one with a snaphaunce and two with flint-locks of the very earliest form, dating from the first quarter of the seventeenth century. Perhaps the most interesting is the small wheel-lock gun (No. 25, Plate X) which must have been made for the King during his childhood between 1610 and 1615. It has the characteristic wide flat butt of the late sixteenth century, but the three muskets from the Cabinet d'Armes (Nos. M4, 5 and 6–1949) have already the club-shaped stock which is the prototype of the modern gunstock. Though it is not stamped with an Inventory number of the Cabinet d'Armes, the holster pistol No. 32, Plate XV is believed to have come from the Paris Arsenal and in view of its technical interest—it is equipped with a left- and right-hand lock arranged to fire two charges consecutively, one placed in front of the other—may well have been made for the French King.

While the French gunsmiths had perfected the true flint-lock during the early years of the seventeenth century, the Italian gunsmiths kept to the wheel-lock. The early Italian wheel-lock is almost indistinguishable from the South German prototype from which it was copied, but the gunsmiths of Northern Italy, mainly in Brescia and the valleys around that city, developed a particularly handsome form of pierced and chiselled steel work which has made their productions the most sought after of all seventeenth-century fire-arms. The Museum collections include a good series of Brescian firearms showing the various techniques of ornament executed in both steel and brass. The most delicate of the Brescian work is found in the flat panels of steel which were pierced and engraved with designs of animals, birds, monsters and figures enclosed within florid Baroque foliate scrollwork. This technique is well illustrated in the ornament of the wheel-lock pistol (No. 45, Plate XVIII). The Brescian steel-workers also displayed surpassing skill in chiselling figures in high relief, as in the snaphaunce lock (No. 48, Plate XX). Alongside the high technical proficiency of the Brescian steel-workers, one finds craftsmen in villages widely spread in North Italy producing similar locks with much high-relief chiselling, coarsely executed with a rustic naiveté. The North Italian craftsmen were, fortunately, in the practice of signing their productions so it is usually possible to attribute pieces to particular masters. Moreover, the various craftsmen who worked on the production of a firearm signed the parts for which they were individually responsible. It is usual to find a barrel-smith's signature and a locksmith's signature on an Italian firearm. In some cases the maker of the mounts or of the stock has added his signature as well. About the middle of the seventeenth century a form of snaphaunce lock replaced the wheel-lock in Northern Italy. This development gave exceptional opportunity to the Brescian craftsmen who were able to chisel both the cock and the arm of the steel in the round in the form of human figures or monsters. It is interesting to note that whereas the characteristic low relief chiselled ornament of the Brescian gunstock mounters was entirely indigenous, the design of some of the chiselled cocks seems to have been derived from the pattern book of François Marcou, published in Paris about the middle of the seventeenth century. The splendour of the Italian steel-chiselling was widely recognized in the seventeenth century, and most of the European princes, including Louis XIII of France, acquired examples for their collections. The Brescian genius lay rather in fine steel working and, in particular, in cutting the surface of the gun stocks with extraordinary precision to receive the pierced steel tracery, than in the technical qualities of lock-making; and a Brescian lock, seen from the inside, shows little of the precision of the best German or French locks of the same period. Those who could not afford a Brescian pistol had a pair of Brescian barrels mounted up by a local gunmaker, and there was a considerable export trade in finished barrels from Brescia. Most of the Brescian barrels were stamped with the name Lazarino Cominazzo, perhaps more by way of a trade mark than a signature, for it seems hardly possible that all the barrels signed in this way could have been produced in one workshop. The Cominazzo family, of which several generations made gun barrels, sent them abroad in bundles ready for mounting, but it has been suggested that they may have delivered others in the rough and hence without the Cominazzo signature. This might have been stamped on the barrels after finishing by the gunmaker who had ordered them. This theory would account for the many variant forms in which the Cominazzo signature is found. There is, on the other hand, no doubt that many barrel-smiths outside Italy fraudulently stamped the Cominazzo signature on their own productions in order to take advantage of the high reputation of the Cominazzo name. Though the members of the Cominazzo family were pre-eminently barrel-smiths, they also assembled and sold fire-arms, as we know from the often cited passage in Evelyn's diary in which he states that he bought a fine carbine of 'old Lazarino Cominazzo'. These carbines, which were intended to be carried at the saddle-bow, are represented by a very fine example in the Museum with two cocks (pyrites holders) (No. R.U.S.I. 2). The iron pyrites which was used to produce the sparks to ignite the priming powder was a much softer material than the flint that was used with the snaphaunce or flint-lock systems and a reserve cock with a second piece of pyrites was likely to be of use in emergency.

The North Italian locksmiths, having abandoned the wheel-lock shortly before the middle of the seventeenth century, adopted the French type of lock in which the main-spring was placed on the inside of the lock-plate and the scear worked vertically, engaging in a recess cut in the tumbler. This mechanism was combined at first with the snaphaunce system by which the pancover and steel (battery or frizzen) were independent elements connected only by a link. Very soon after, possibly at the same time, the true flint lock frizzen was introduced, in which the battery and the pancover were combined in one. The two types continued in use in North Italy up to the end of the seventeenth century, and even later. The snaphaunce system with independent pancover and battery, though less compact and requiring an extra motion in loading, had the advantage that no safety catch was required on the cocking mechanism, since the lock could be made secure when cocked and primed by turning back the battery.

In Southern Italy a type of chiselled ornament was adopted, by comparison with which even the florid Brescian style seems restrained. The lock was chiselled with grotesque masks carved in very high relief, and with figure sculpture executed in the round. This style of ornament has been associated with Naples, mainly because somewhat similar designs are found on the cup hilts of rapiers signed by Neapolitan masters. The lock with two cocks (172–1869) shows it in its most extreme taste. When the wheel-lock was given up, the gunmakers of Central and South Italy adopted the so-called *Miquelet* or Mediterranean lock. This was an improved version of the German-Dutch snaphaunce of the sixteenth century. It was evolved in Spain during the first half of the seventeenth century and may have entered Italy through the Spanish rulers of Naples and Southern Italy, though a direct connection between Italian and Northern gunmakers cannot be excluded. The *Miquelet* lock in both its Spanish and Italian versions had a frizzen in which battery and pancover were combined, thus improving on the sixteenth-century snaphaunce. The *Miquelet* lock continued in use both in Italy and Spain until the late eighteenth century, and, in rare cases, even into the nineteenth century. The Museum has an extensive collection of Italian gunlocks of northern and southern types and all the mechanisms referred to above are represented in numerous versions. Particularly noteworthy are the locks No. 48 (Plate XX), M.546–1924 signed by Michele Lorenzoni of Florence, and M.498–1937, signed by Domenico Santi of Montealboddo.

The existence of numbers of unmounted locks of Italian origin is doubtless due to the fact that gunmakers ordered them in quantity from the locksmiths and they were held in stock until needed. These examples were probably overtaken by some change in fashion or technical improvement before ever being mounted.

During the second quarter of the seventeenth century, a fashion for austerity in design and decoration of firearms became apparent in Germany and in Western Europe. Instead of the elaborately inlaid stocks which had been popular in the Low Countries, Northern France and Germany, we find stocks of ebony or of a soft wood stained and varnished to resemble ebony. Instead of the chiselled, blued and gilt mounts found on the finest German firearms, the mounts are restricted to bands around the butt and the fore-end, made of thin sheet silver or of gilt copper, engraved with some appropriate design. The silver-mounted group is represented in the Museum by a pair (No. 31, Plate XI) while the pair of pistols (No. 30, Plate XI) with mounts of gilt copper show another aspect of this trend towards sobriety in ornament. It was only in the larger gunmaking centres of Europe that such changes in fashion had any real effect. In the peripheral territories, in Italy, Spain and Poland, they passed unnoticed. The court workshop of the Electors of Bavaria continued also to work in the same manner as had been devised by Emanuel Sadeler some thirty years earlier.

While the elaborate bone inlay on gunstocks was becoming old-fashioned in Western Germany by the middle of the seventeenth century, in the east of Germany and in Poland, it had a much longer life. One particular school of gunmakers produced a wide variety of firearms, all decorated in similar manner. They are not signed, nor is there any barrel-smith's stamp on the barrels, so it is not possible to be precise about their source. The stocks are profusely but coarsely inlaid with engraved bone and mother of pearl. The locks and barrels are decorated with panels of gilt punched work, the remaining surface being blued. The Museum collection includes two Tschinkes (No. 33, Plate XIII) a wheel-lock rifle (M.101–1930) and a flint-lock holster pistol (No. 59, Plate XXV) all decorated in the same manner and evidently dating from the second half of the seventeenth century. Though there is no internal evidence to show that these firearms came from Eastern Germany or Poland, there is in the Swedish Royal Armoury at Stockholm a number of wheel-lock rifles which show the same scheme of ornament on the barrels, namely punched and gilt panels, alternating with blued panels. These rifles are known to have been brought from Mitau in Courland. A flint-lock rifle in the Museum (M.228–1919) dating from the third quarter of the seventeenth century and of Russian origin, has a stock of German type, coarsely inlaid with bone, and looks at first sight like a village-made German gun. It has the long butt characteristic of wheel-lock firearms of East German provenance.

When the South German gunmakers abandoned bone inlay during the second half of the seventeenth century, they turned to other forms of ornament. The stocks were carved with figure subjects or scrollwork (7821–1861), inlaid with steel wire (M.637–1927), or overlaid with plaques of ivory. A series of firearms with stocks overlaid with plaques of ivory carved in such high relief as to make them more suitable for the Kunstkabinett than the chase were made by the Swabian carver, Michael Maucher, for the Electors of Bavaria. A similar rifle, also signed by Maucher, from the Museum collection is shown in Plate XIII, No. 50. It has the additional feature of being a breech-loading arm, and must have been intended for use in spite of the delicate nature of the ornament. The wheel-lock continued in use as a sporting and target weapon in Germany long after it had been abandoned elsewhere. The latest example in the Museum (No. 64, Plate XXVIII) dates from the early years of the eighteenth century, but there are a number of finely chiselled detached locks which were probably made as late as the second quarter of the eighteenth century (No. 62, Plate XVII). During the early decades of the eighteenth century, steel chiselling of very high quality was produced by a number of craftsmen working in Bavaria and in Austria. There is a representative series of these wheel-locks in the Museum, the best examples bear the signatures of Nicolaus Koch of Vienna and C. Ofner of Innsbruck respectively (M.538–1924 and No. 62, Plate XVII). The latter is of particular interest in that it is also signed by the chiseller with his initials I.M.K. The wars of liberation against the Turks often provide themes for the decoration of the locks from Eastern Europe. The lock of the Christoph Frey rifle (No. 64, Plate XXVIII) is chiselled and engraved with a combat scene between European and Turkish cavalry, while the detached wheel-lock (719–1877), signed by M. Muck of Brunn in Moravia, is engraved with a representation of the defeat of the Turks before the walls of Belgrade on 22 August 1717. About the middle of the seventeenth century, the form of the wheel-lock was changed in that the wheel was accommodated on the interior, instead of the exterior, of the lock

(No. 64, Plate XXVIII). This alteration was not by any means generally applied, and locks of sixteenth-century date had often been enclosed with a domed cover (No. 8, Plate IV). A more streamlined effect is achieved on a lock (M.537–1924) dating from the third quarter of the seventeenth century, signed Georg Kog (presumably Georg Koch of Vienna). Here the cock spring as well as the wheel are accommodated on the interior of the lock-plate and the arm of the cock is flattened so that it is flush with the lock face. This last lock is very finely engraved with hunting subjects enclosed within foliage derived from the 'Neues Groteschgen Büchlein' of the Prague engraver Johann Schmischek, a work which was much in favour as a source for the ornament of gun-furniture. The steel chisellers of the Munich school also made use of this particular pattern book as a source for their gun ornament about the middle of the seventeenth century.

It is, perhaps, no coincidence that the supremacy of the French gunmakers in the latter part of the seventeenth century corresponded in time with the dominating position of France under the rule of Louis XIV in European politics. An indication of the importance attached to fine firearms in the seventeenth century can be gained from the fact that when, in 1673, Louis XIV wished to make a splendid gift to Charles XI, King of Sweden, he presented him with a series of firearms, all by the foremost Parisian gunsmiths, in addition to twelve richly caparisoned horses. Six guns, five brace of pistols and one single pistol from this gift are still preserved in the Stockholm Royal Armoury.

In judging the merit of design in firearms, one is inevitably more concerned with the applied ornament than with questions of form. Though the gunsmith has always been compelled by practical and technical considerations to adhere to a closely defined form, he can, through his ability or failure to exercise a sense of plastic form, produce a beautiful or an exceedingly graceless object. A comparison between any so-called Levantine pistol and the examples illustrated in Plate XVIII will demonstrate this fact.

As long as gunstocks had been inlaid with horn, there had been little appreciation of the natural qualities of the wood of which the stocks were composed. About the middle of the seventeenth century, wood stocks were covered with ivory or with tortoiseshell, or stained to resemble ebony, but little attempt was made to exploit the figure of the wood. The main exceptions to this rule were the stocks of palisander or other exotic wood which were constructed by the Munich gunstockers, Hieronymus Borstorffer, father and son, for the guns decorated by the Sadelers. During the third quarter of the seventeenth century, we find stocks made of finely-figured walnut. The Parisian gunmakers were probably the first to appreciate the decorative possibilities of a finely-figured stock, but the fashion spread rapidly across Europe, and the Museum can show examples from England in the West to Eger in Sudetenland in the East. It is true that inlay of silver wire is found on the finest stocks of the late seventeenth century, but this was rarely so profuse as to obscure the figure of the wood.

It was not easy to find pieces of finely-figured wood of dimensions large enough to provide a gun or even a pistol stock, and if the stocks are carefully examined, they will often be found to have been pieced together. The figure was artificially heightened by slightly charring the surface over a flame, which gave the contrast between light and dark that is so characteristic of the late seventeenth century. The stocks of the finest guns were made of root walnut, while maple was used for the cheaper lines.

A feature of French firearms of the seventeenth century, particularly of the middle decades, was the fine engraved ornament with which the steel parts were decorated. The finest work was done by Jacquinet, who engraved the copper-plates of the two books of gunmakers' ornament issued by François Marcou and Thuraine et Le Hollandois about 1650–60 (Plates XIV and XVII). Unfortunately, engraving on steel is very easily destroyed through rust oxidization and few guns have survived outside the hereditary armouries of the European royal families, which show this engraved ornament in anything approaching its original condition. There are, on the other hand, a great many pulls taken from engraved lockplates or mounts of firearms in the Department of Engraving, Illustration and Design. Some of these are illustrated in Plate XVI and show the engraving in its original state. The ornament consisted at first of grotesque monsters amidst foliage and hunting subjects. Subsequently, during the reign of Louis XIV (No. 42, Plate XVI), subjects drawn from classical history were increasingly employed. The lock-plates of the mid-seventeenth century were flat and offered therefore a most suitable surface for engraving. Between 1660 and 1670 Parisian fashion favoured lock-plates with a rounded surface, and the latter form remained fashionable until the end of the century. Provincial and foreign gunmakers were slower to follow a new fashion than those of the capital city of France, but through the medium of the pattern books, the Paris fashions became known and were emulated throughout Europe.

En suite with the lock-plate, the other mounts, side-plate, trigger guard and escutcheon were after about 1660 executed in relief instead of in the flat. This development very much restricted the scope of the engraver but it did on the other hand create new opportunities for the steel chiseller. After the introduction of the rounded forms, we find finely chiselled steel mounts being produced all over Western Europe. Examples in the Museum collections of this period are signed by makers in London, Turin, Sedan and Liége. One of the most attractive features of the firearms of the second half of the seventeenth and the first half of the eighteenth centuries was the exploitation of the decorative possibilites of the side-plate, the strip of metal set into the stock on the side opposite to the lock. Its function was merely to prevent the lock-screws (in English gunmaking terminology, side nails), which had to be very firmly screwed up, from biting into the wood of the stock. In this period we find it rendered in most attractive combinations of Baroque foliate scrollwork, human figures, serpents, etc. (No. 43, Plate XVI).

The dating of the flint locks of the second half of the seventeenth century can be established by reference to the degree of elaboration in the design of the side-plate and the form of the frizzen (fire-steel or battery). The breast of the frizzen of the mid-seventeenth century is carved with a single acanthus leaf, subsequently a small wart-like projection is substituted. As the century advanced, this wart develops foliation and finally assumes a form resembling the conventional representation of a bomb.

During the second half of the seventeenth century and the early eighteenth century, the Parisian pattern books secured so widespread a distribution that an international style of design grew up, based on Parisian prototypes. Even in Spain and Italy, which had hitherto remained consistently faithful to their national styles, gunmakers made use of the two Simonin pattern books published in Paris in 1685 and 1693. An outstanding example is the three-barrelled revolving pistol by Michele Lorenzoni of Florence (No. 56, Plate XXVI) which might at first sight pass for the work of a Parisian master. In the early eighteenth century, the force of Parisian fashion was so strongly felt that we find gunmakers all over Northern Europe signing their locks in French, as in the case of the very French-looking piece from the armoury of the Grand Duke Ernst August of Saxe-Weimar, signed 'Tanner à Gotha 1724' (No. 73, Plate XXVIII).

Many fine firearms were produced in the seventeenth century on the north-eastern borders of France in the province of Lorraine, particularly in the city of Metz. During the second half of the century there was an important gunmaking industry in the northern French town of Sedan, where such distinguished makers as Ezechias Colas, Daniel Martin, Gabriel Gourinal and Soiron were at work. The last of these makers is represented by a finely-chiselled flint-lock holster pistol (M.11–1949). Until 1642 Sedan was the capital of an independent principality of the Dukes of Bouillon, Princes of Sedan, and was a flourishing centre of the crafts. After its incorporation in the kingdom of France in that year its importance waned, and the Revocation of the Edict of Nantes in 1685 drove away its craftsmen, reducing it to the status of a provincial town. It was not only in the northern provinces that fine firearms were produced; there was also an important gunmaking school at Angers. Dr. Lenk records in *Flintlåset* a number of most splendid firearms, signed by Monlong, Martin and Boular, each of whom was at the time working in Angers.

The high quality of the French provincial gunmakers was less marked in the eighteenth century, possibly because some of the most distinguished of the provincials had taken up residence in Paris. A gunmaker signing himself 'Le Lorrain à Valence', who had evidently left the province of Lorraine and moved to the south, is represented by quite a good quality holster pistol dating from the last decade of the seventeenth century (M.10–1949).

About the middle of the seventeenth century a group of pistols with finely-chiselled mounts made in Liége emerges. The locks, barrels and mounts are chiselled with battle scenes or with profile heads in costume of the mid-seventeenth century; in order to provide the maximum space for chiselled ornament the frizzen spring is fixed to the inside of the lock-plate. Of this group, the Museum possesses a detached lock (M.547–1924) the chiselled ornament after Marcou, a detached barrel (M.687–1927) and a single pistol, signed 'Fabri à Liége' (M.9–1949). This last piece is one of the later examples of the group, dating from *circa* 1670–80. It still has, however, the characteristic profile heads chiselled on the pommel, and the fact that it is signed by a Liége maker gives it documentary value as the earlier examples in the group are all unsigned, and have, for this reason, not hitherto been attributed to any definite place of origin. The Liége gunmakers produced work of high quality during the seventeenth and eighteenth centuries and further examples from Liége workshops will be referred to below.

Few references have hitherto been made to English gunmaking, not because it did not exist, but because its earlier phases are not represented in the Museum. Some of the most important of the gunmakers working in England in the seventeenth century were foreign immigrants; Harman Barne, gunmaker to Prince Rupert and later to Charles II, and Kaspar Kalthoff, assistant to the Earl of Worcester in his famous experiments and inventor of a breech-loading magazine rifle, were both Germans; Monlong was of French origin, presumably of Huguenot faith, and Dolep, gunmaker to Lord Dartmouth, was a Dutchman.

The Civil War in England led to a great interest in accurate military weapons, and the so-called 'turn-off' gun or pistol was developed to meet this demand. This type is represented in the Museum by a flint-lock holster pistol, signed Fisher, probably a provincial gunmaker, dating from about 1680 (No. 61, Plate XXIV). The barrel, which is rifled, unscrews at the breech, permitting the charge and bullet to be inserted directly in the chamber. A bullet of diameter very slightly larger than the bore of the barrel was employed, thus ensuring, firstly, that the ball did not leave the chamber until the charge was fully ignited, and secondly that it fitted the barrel so closely that it could not fail to take the rifling. These pistols took a very heavy charge, the chamber being about the same size as that of a modern service rifle. In order to resist the force of the discharge, the walls of the barrel were made of thicker metal than those of contemporary muzzle-loading pistols, and the walls of the reinforce may be as much as $\frac{5}{16}$ in. thick. It has been credibly suggested that these rifled pistols were designed to pierce the so-called bullet-proof breastplates which were still worn by cuirassiers during the Civil Wars. Technically, they were more efficient than any of the muzzle-loading firearms produced in England during the first three-quarters of the eighteenth century. During the hundred years from about 1680 to 1780, there seems to have been little interest in devising pistols which could achieve high velocity and therefore, accuracy and power of penetration. Most of the seventeenth-century rifled pistols were full-length holster pistols intended for use by cavalry and the reason for their desuetude may have been an alteration in the tactical handling of mounted troops involving the substitution of charging with the sword for long-distance firing. It is probable that this system was developed and perfected in England. The earliest known English example, dating from about 1650, is signed by Harman Barne, and there is no doubt that they were more popular in England than elsewhere. Dutch, French and Austrian examples are known—the last combined with wheel-lock ignition—but they are far more rare than those by English makers. It is a surprising fact that no example of the screwed barrel is shown in the French gunmakers' pattern books of the mid-seventeenth century; this circumstance shows that there can have been little demand for them on the Continent at the time. This system retained its popularity in England throughout the eighteenth century, but mainly for small-size pistols with smooth-bore barrels. The eighteenth-century type is represented by the Turvey pistol (No. 70, Plate XXIV). The eighteenth-century examples were not military pistols, but were intended for personal protection. They lack therefore the feature of the Fisher pistol, namely the link which attached the barrel to the stock when unscrewed and thus made loading on horseback possible.

While the Kalthoff family had been the first to develop an effective breech-loading magazine system, English gunmakers were probably unable to produce the forgings necessary for its manufacture. Another system, the invention of which is usually attributed to the Florentine gunmaker Michele Lorenzoni, was adopted by several English makers. It is represented in the Museum by a particularly fine example, signed by John Cookson of London (No. 54, Plate XXII). A repeating system, possibly identical with that of this gun was patented in 1664 by the London gunmaker, Abraham Hill. Magazine guns of this type were produced by other London gunsmiths about the 1670's and 1680's evidently without regard to Hill's patent. During the eighteenth century this system was occasionally used on pistols. A characteristic Birmingham-made pocket pistol, the lock with the spurious signature 'London', dating from about 1780 (M.683–1927) shows a simplified version of the system.

The end of the seventeenth century saw a turn of fashion away from the rounded surfaces introduced about forty years earlier. Two Parisian pattern books by Nicholas Guérard and de Lacollombe (Nos. 66 and 71) respectively helped to disseminate the new ideas throughout Western Europe. At the same time convenience and economy led to the use of less decorative but more solid walnut stocks instead of the very short grained burr and root wood which had been employed for all the best quality weapons. The fact that a number of fine-quality pistols of seventeenth-century date have been restocked in the eighteenth century in plain straight-grained walnut testifies to the short life of the more decorative burr wood stocks. Another innovation was the gilding of the ground of the chiselled steel on the best-quality pieces. These three developments wrought a great change in the flint-lock gun or pistol, which became considerably more sumptuous in appearance. Its ornament was now immediately obvious to the eye and no longer needed to be sought out. The Régence ornament which is found in the Guérard and De Lacollombe pattern books was derived from the designs of Jean Berain the Younger. Consisting of strapwork, acanthus foliage, trophies of arms and grotesque masks, it was peculiarly suitable for application to firearms. At the same time, something of the elegance of line, which had been sacrificed when the plumper forms and relief carving of the Simonin style was adopted, was recovered, at any rate by the Parisian gunsmiths. The Museum collections do not as yet include a fine Parisian piece of the early eighteenth century, but the effect of the new style can be studied in firearms made outside France under the influence of the new pattern books. The brace of holster pistols signed by I. I. Behr (No. 68, Plate XXX), no town of origin given, but attributable on internal evidence to Liége, show a western version of the style, while a Southern European version can be seen in the single holster pistol made in the Royal Armoury of the Kings of Sardinia at Turin (No. 75, Plate XXX). The same style, but with engraved instead of chiselled ornament, and showing the purest Parisian manner is represented by the fowling-piece made by a member of the Tanner family for the Saxon court (No. 73, Plate XXVIII). The mounts of the last mentioned are of silver, a metal which was much more extensively used for gun furniture about the close of the seventeenth century. This meant a great saving in labour for the gunmakers, for whereas the steel mounts had to be forged, filed to shape and finally chiselled and engraved, silver mounts were cast, and, if necessary, slightly chiselled and then they were ready for use. In England, the gunmaker did not make silver mounts, but bought them in quantity from silversmiths in London and Birmingham who specialized in their manufacture. The grotesque mask butt on the screw-barrelled pistol by W. Turvey (No. 70, Plate XXIV) is, for instance, of a standard type that was used by most of the eighteenth-century gunmakers in London for this class of weapon. Until about 1780 silver was increasingly employed for better quality arms, particularly in England, where great skill was shown in combining delicate silver inlay work in the wood stocks with rather massive silver mounts. One of the most magnificent examples of this technique of ornament is the air-gun signed by Kolbe and believed to have been made for George II (No. 78, Plates XXXI–XXXIII). Kolbe was, as his name suggests, a German and there is no doubt that this air-gun was made only shortly after he left his home town of Suhl for England. Nevertheless the chiselling and embossing of the silver of the mounts must be the work of English craftsmen, for they are of a quality beyond that likely to be achieved by even the most gifted of gunmakers. It is probable that Kolbe called in the assistance of a watch-case maker to carry out the silver-work. The great weight of the silver ornament on this gun makes it, incidentally, heavy and clumsy to use. Its decoration is not copied slavishly from a pattern book but has been designed individually. This Kolbe air-gun is an exceptional weapon made for a royal patron, but the same elements of ornament, employed on a less lavish scale, could produce particularly attractive results, as on the fowling-piece by Wilson of 1749 (No. 76, Plate XXXI) or the cannon-barrelled pistol by W. Turvey (No. 70, Plate XXIV).

A particularly unusual pair of pistols by the Liége maker, Devillers, have stocks entirely of silver (No. 69, Plate XXV). They are of the cannon-barrel type and are rifled but there is no provision for the barrels to unscrew. They point to the high quality of Liége gun-making in the first half of the eighteenth century. Subsequently, the Liége makers seem to have concentrated on the production of military and trade guns. While in France and England silver mounts were much favoured, in the Low Countries, in Southern Germany, in Austria and in what is now Czecho-Slovakia, mounts of gilt brass or ormolu were more usual. The finest work in this material was done by the gunmakers of Austria and of Bavaria, and firearms made for the German princes have mounts of brass or bronze, cast and then finely chiselled and gilt. The use of gilt brass, which contrasted most effectively with the walnut stocks, coincided in period with the last phases of Baroque art in Central Europe. We find the late Baroque motives of interlacing strapwork, delicate acanthus foliage and figure subjects taken from classical mythology fully exploited in the design of these mounts. A wheel-lock rifle from Munich (No. 64, Plate XXVIII) shows the South German style, while a pair of pistols (No. 67, Plate XXV) and a flint-lock rifle (M192–1951) show the slightly coarser but colourful manner of the Bohemian workshops. The popularity of gilt brass mounts in the Low Countries can be attributed, at any rate as far as the Austrian Netherlands were concerned, to Austrian influence. It is interesting to note that the pair of Liége pistols (No. 69, Plate XXV) were made for a Hungarian nobleman. The use of gilt brass or bronze in Liége and in Central Europe must be distinguished from the practice in England. Here it was, throughout the eighteenth century, reserved for second-quality arms.

The Museum is fortunate in possessing outstanding examples of the gunsmiths' art of France and Germany as well as of England, dating from the middle years of the eighteenth century. The pistols (No. 79, Plates XXIX and XXX) were made for Louis XV, King of France and must be amongst the most richly ornamented firearms in existence. They belong to the late Rococo period of about 1750–60 when rather inappropriate sprigs of naturalistic flowers were beginning to intrude amongst the flame-like scrolls of the earlier and purer style. Their creator has exploited every available technique of ornament, but in spite of this ornament that runs riot over their surface, they have a beauty of form that is worthy of the great traditions of Parisian gunmaking. It is essential to remember their colour scheme, the lock and mounts of bright steel, against a gold ground, the barrels partly encrusted with gold against a brilliant blue ground, and finally the inlay of gold wire in the richly-figured walnut stocks.

The Saxon court had always been great patrons of the makers of fine arms and armour, and in the eighteenth century they gave many commissions for firearms to the family of Stockmar, three members of which held in succession the office of *Hofgraveur* at the Saxon court. The Stockmars were one of the few gunmaking families who succeeded in realizing some of the more extravagant ideas of the French designers of the eighteenth century. The Rococo style gave unlimited scope for improvisation, and the Stockmar guns are not drawn literally from the pattern book. Not all their fantasies are to be admired—for example the stocks of the garniture in the Wallace Collection, which are decorated with stags' teeth. While Stockmar's designs include figure subjects, the main element consists of the flame-like motifs that are so typical of German rococo. These are chiselled in the steel mounts against a matt gold ground, carved in the walnut stock, and inlaid in silver wire. The fowling piece (No. 77, Plate XXVIII) shows their style at its best.

During the second half of the eighteenth century, numerous improvements in the methods of manufacture of gun barrels and in the design of the lock made the flint-lock a highly efficient weapon. It was not till about 1770 that the English gunsmiths reintroduced the flat lock-plate which had been adopted on the Continent at the turn of the century. During the last two or three decades of the century, the practice of duelling with the pistol was introduced, and a pair of duelling pistols seems to have been a necessary part of the equipment of a gentleman. As the technical effectiveness of the firearm increased, its decorative qualities ceased to be of importance. Instead of chiselled and gilt steel, silver or ormolu, the mounts were made of blued steel which had the practical advantage of not reflecting the light, but offered little scope for ornament. During the seventeenth century and the first three quarters of the eighteenth century, English gunmakers had not enjoyed any great fame outside the British Isles, but the advent of the duelling pistol gave them an opportunity which they did not fail to take. The English duelling pistol was a weapon of extreme accuracy and its lock-work was made with a precision which had never before been achieved in the history of firearms; its development during the last years of the eighteenth century is associated with names such as D. Egg, H. W. Mortimer and the Mantons. Firearms of this type hardly find a place in a Museum of applied art but the last phase of the flint-lock in England is represented by a pair of double-barrelled pocket pistols signed by Joseph Egg, London and bearing the London Hallmark for 1823 (No. 81, Plate XXXIX). These pistols are of the very highest quality as regards both construction and finish. That they were highly regarded is evident from the fact that they are partly mounted in gold. An interesting feature is the presence of the mainspring on the outside of the lock. This was not a new development and had been introduced for double-barrelled under and over pistols during the first half of the eighteenth century. By placing the mainsprings in this position the width of the pistols could be reduced so that they might more conveniently be accommodated in the pocket.

In France, Nicholas Noel Boutet, Director of the Arms Factory at Versailles under Louis XVI and subsequently during the Directoire and Empire periods, succeeded in applying many features from the rich stock of Empire ornament to his firearms. His productions, most of which were presentation weapons for Napoleonic officers or for foreign princes, were of the highest artistic merit, but he is at present only represented in the Museum collections by a sword.

J.F.H.

SHORT BIBLIOGRAPHY

BOEHEIM, W. *Meister der Waffenschmiedekunst.* Berlin, 1897.

DRUMMOND, J. *Ancient Scottish Weapons.* London, 1881.

GEORGE, J. H. *English Pistols and Revolvers.* Plantersville, U.S.A., 1938.

GEORGE, J. H. *English Guns and Rifles.* Plantersville, U.S.A., 1947.

GERMANISCHES MUSEUM. *Quellen zur Geschichte der Feuerwaffen.* 2 vols. Leipzig, 1872–77.

GRANCSAY, S. V. *Master French Gunsmith's Designs.* New York, 1950.

HOFF, A. *Aeldre Dansk Bøssemageri.* 2 vols. Copenhagen, 1951.

JACKSON, H. J. and WHITELAW, C.E. *European Hand Firearms, with a treatise on Scottish Hand Firearms.* London, 1923.

LENK, T. *Flintlåset.* Stockholm, 1939.

MEYERSON, A. *Stockholms Bössmakare.* Stockholm, 1936.

POLLARD, H. B. C. *A History of Firearms.* London, 1930.

SCHEDELMANN, H. *Die Wiener Büchsenmacher und Büchsenschäfter. Beiheft der Zeitschrift f. hist. Waffenkunde.* Berlin, 1944.

STØCKEL, J. F. *Haandskydevaabens Bedømmelse.* 2 vols. Copenhagen, 1938–43.

STÖCKLEIN, H. *Meister des Eisenschnittes.* Esslingen, 1922.

THIERBACH, M. *Die Geschichtliche Entwicklung der Handfeuerwaffen.* 3 vols. Dresden, 1886.

APPENDIX: DESCRIPTION OF MECHANISMS
USED FROM THE
SIXTEENTH TO EIGHTEENTH CENTURIES

THE MATCH-LOCK (*Fig. 1*)

The match-lock consisted of a forked match-holder or serpentine (A), in which the slow match was fixed by means of a small thumb-screw (B), and a lever or scear (C) pivoted upon the inside of the lock-plate and linked to the serpentine in such a manner that when its hindmost end was raised the serpentine was made to swing with a circular motion, bringing the lighted end of the match down upon the flash-pan. This was filled with fine gunpowder and communicated with the charge in the barrel by means of a small vent or touch-hole bored through the side wall of the breech. The scear and serpentine were set in motion by means of a long trigger, similar in form to that of a crossbow, which acted on the hindmost end of the scear, whilst a scear-spring (D), screwed or pinned to the inside of the lock-plate, and pressing against the foremost end of the scear, served to hold the lighted match clear of the flash-pan until the trigger was pressed. The flash-pan was at first a part not of the lock but of the barrel, being either brazed or welded into its breech. It was protected by a hinged pan-cover, which served to hold the priming in position. This was swung open horizontally immediately before firing.

When loading, the first motion was to remove the match from the serpentine, and to grasp it in the left hand, the lighted ends being kept well away from the powder during the process of loading. The piece was then 'ordered', the musketeer placing the butt upon the ground and holding the barrel in his left hand, while with his right he took his powder flask of coarse gunpowder from his waist-belt and measured out a charge of gunpowder. This operation was performed by holding the flask upside down and pressing a thumb-catch which allowed an exact charge of powder to flow into the nozzle. Then, releasing the thumb-catch and pressing another catch which opened the mouth of the nozzle, he poured the charge into the barrel of his musket following it up with a fragment of wadding, and a bullet taken from his pouch, and finally ramming the charge home with a stroke of his ramrod, which he withdrew from its slot in the musket stock for this purpose.

These preliminaries completed, it remained only to prime the piece, filling its flash-pan with a fine-grained powder from his priming flask, closing the pan and blowing away any loose powder from the cover. He then returned the match to the serpentine and fixed it with a turn of the thumbscrew. The piece was then ready for discharge. If the musketeer was not able to discharge his piece immediately, it was necessary for him to readjust frequently his match in the serpentine so that the projecting end should be of the right length to fall squarely in the pan upon his pressing the trigger, and sometimes to re-light the match from its other end, which was kept burning for this purpose, if it should burn down to the serpentine and go out.

During the sixteenth century, the match 'tricker' lock was introduced. This was an improvement on the first form of match-lock. In this case, the flash-pan, the pan-cover and a shield (E) intended to protect the eye of the musketeer from the flash of his priming were attached to the lock. Further, the scear and the serpentine were set in motion by a separate trigger, which was protected by a trigger guard in the modern fashion (*Fig. 2*).

THE WHEEL-LOCK (*Fig. 3*)

In the wheel-lock the lighted match is dispensed with, the priming being ignited by means of a piece of iron pyrites (A), held in contact with the serrated edge of a steel wheel (B), which is rotated by means of a powerful 'V' mainspring (C) attached to the inner side of the lock-plate. In order to prepare the lock for firing, it is necessary to fit a key upon the squared end of the spindle (D) on which this wheel revolved, and to turn the spindle in a clockwise direction, winding up a short steel chain (E) which connects the spindle with the free end of the mainspring. When three-quarters of a revolution have been completed, a scear (F) fixed upon the inside of the lock-plate engages in a recess cut in the inner surface of the wheel and so secures it in position, with the spring bent and the chain wound tightly round the spindle (D). The flash-pan (H), which is attached to the lock-plate and pierced at the bottom to admit the serrated edge of the wheel, is then primed in the usual manner, the pan-cover (I) closed, and the dog-head (J) holding in its jaws a piece of iron-pyrites lowered so that it rests on the upper surface of the pan-cover. It is held in contact with the latter by means of a strong spring (K). When the trigger is pressed, it draws back the scear horizontally, freeing the wheel. The latter, impelled by the force of the mainspring, begins to turn rapidly, and at the same time a cam attached to the spindle strikes violently against a steel arm (L) pivoting at its lower end on the lower part of the lock-plate and attached at its upper end to the pan-cover. The arm is forced back, drawing back the pan-cover and allowing the piece of iron-pyrites to fall upon the serrated edge of the wheel as it revolves at full speed, striking a shower of sparks and igniting the priming powder in the flash-pan. The pan-cover itself is secured in the open position by a spring catch (M) and so held until the pan is re-primed.

THE DUTCH OR GERMAN SNAPHAUNCE (*Fig. 4*)

In the Dutch or German version of the snaphaunce lock, the cock (A), bearing a piece of flint in its jaws, strikes upon a steel (B), thus producing a spark to ignite the priming. In order to prepare the piece for discharge, the pan (C) is primed, the pan-cover closed and the cock drawn back to 'set' position. The Dutch snaphaunce scear (D) does not (as was the case with the later locks) engage in a notch cut upon a tumbler, but projects through the lock-plate, as does the scear of the wheel-lock, and acts directly upon the cock, catching upon a lug or tail or engaging in a slot cut in its inner face (E). No half-cock is provided, since it is possible for the snaphaunce piece to be carried, when fully primed and loaded, with its cock set, but with its steel raised clear of the flash-pan, in which position it is impossible for the lock to give fire by accident. To prepare the piece for discharge it is sufficient to lower the steel on to the pan-cover. When the trigger is pressed, the scear is withdrawn horizontally through the opening in the lock-plate, freeing the tail of the cock, which is forced down upon the steel by the action of the main-spring (F). The mainspring is placed inside the lock, and exerts its force on the cock by means of the tumbler (G), a steel block keyed or pinned to the cock-spindle (H) on the inner face of the lock. The tumbler in turn is linked to the pan-cover by an arm (I) on the inner face of the lock. As the tumbler turns, the arm moves over, forcing back the pan-cover at the same time as the flint strikes sparks from the steel.

THE ENGLISH LOCK (*Fig. 5*)

In England a lock was introduced during the first half of the seventeenth century which incorporated the main features of the snaphaunce firing mechanism, in particular the scear acting horizontally through a hole cut in the lock-plate. In this lock the pan-cover is, however, combined with the steel. The combined steel and pan-cover (A) (hammer, battery or frizzen) consists of a hinged cover, working upon a screw set in the lock-plate, and held in position by a light V-spring (B). From the cover a curved steel rises at such an angle that the flint held in the jaws of the cock should strike it with the scraping movement required to produce fire, the pan-cover spring fulfilling the double function of keeping the pan firmly closed until the moment of firing, and causing the pan-cover when struck by the flint to offer sufficient resistance. The sliding pan-cover and also the link connecting it with the tumbler could now be dispensed with, but it was necessary to devise a safety position for the cock to enable the gun to be carried primed and loaded without danger. This safety position consists of a half-cock bent or notch (C) upon the tumbler, in which the scear (D) was engaged when it was desired to set the lock in the half-cock or safety position, with the cock partly raised and the pan closed. In addition to the use of a half-cock bent upon the tumbler a certain number of English locks were fitted with an additional safety device in the form of a hook-shaped catch fixed to the outside of the lock-plate. This catch engages in a recess cut in the tail of the cock when the latter is drawn back just beyond the half-cock position. The catch had to be drawn back with the thumb before the piece could be fired. This form of safety device is commonly called a dog-catch and locks which are so fitted are known as dog-locks. In the later forms of the English flint-lock, dating from the Civil War period, the scear, though still working horizontally, no longer penetrates through the lock-plate but engages in two bents cut in the tumbler. This lock had a very short life in England as it was almost immediately replaced by the French flint-lock. It is not at present represented in the Museum collection.

THE SCANDINAVIAN LOCK (*Fig. 6*)

A variant type of snaphaunce lock was used in Scandinavia where it had a life of some two hundred years from the mid-sixteenth to the mid-eighteenth centuries. In this lock the scear (A) passes horizontally through an aperture in the lock-plate to engage the tail of the cock (B). The mainspring (C) is placed on the interior of the lock-plate and presses down against the tail of the tumbler (F). The pan-cover and steel are separate, the former being opened by hand before firing. There is no half-cock or safety device as the lock can be rendered safe by turning back the steel. On the later examples dating from the second half of the seventeenth century, the steel (E) is screwed to the pan-cover (D) in such a way that it can be turned to one side to provide a safety position. As with the English lock, the later forms of this lock have a tumbler cut with notches, and the scear engages with this when set instead of with the tail of the cock. As the face of the steel could be turned away, there was no need for a safety position for the cock.

THE MEDITERRANEAN LOCK (*Figs. 7 and 8*)

As in the sixteenth-century snaphaunce, the scear operates horizontally through the lock-plate. There are two versions of this lock, the Italian and the Spanish. Both were developed during the first half of the seventeenth century. As the Italian form first appears in South Italy, it is probable that it was an adaptation of the Spanish lock used by the Spanish rulers of the kingdom of Naples. In the Italian version, the scear consists of two arms (A) and (B), the front one of which engages the toe (C) of the cock to provide a half-cock position; while the rear one engages the heel (D) of the cock to provide the full-cock position. When the trigger is pressed both these arms are withdrawn horizontally through the lock-plate, thus allowing the cock to descend under the force of the mainspring (E). The latter is fixed to the exterior of the lock and presses down on the toe of the cock. There is no tumbler. The pan-cover and steel are made in one, hence the necessity for the half-cock position.

The Spanish lock differs from the Italian lock in that the two arms of the scear both pass through the lock-plate in front of the cock (A), the toe of which terminates in a blade (B). The half-cock arm is formed as a stud (C), the full-cock as a flat blade (D), and as the cock is raised the toe engages first with the stud and then with the plate. The mainspring (E) presses up against the heel of the cock. The pan-cover and steel are formed in one, but the latter has a deeply grooved face (F) which is detachable so that it may be easily renewed when worn. The mainsprings on the Spanish locks are often extremely strong, so that the steel probably had a shorter life than was the case with the French flint-lock.

THE FRENCH FLINT-LOCK (*Fig. 9*)

The main feature of the French lock, which was first introduced in the early seventeenth century, and became eventually the standard form in all Northern Europe countries, is the scear (A) operating vertically instead of horizontally. Two bents, half-cock (B) and full-cock (C), are cut in the tumbler (D), and the scear engages with them, instead of passing through the lock-plate to engage with the cock. Apart from the dog-catch which it does not possess, the French lock corresponds in other respects to the English lock described above.

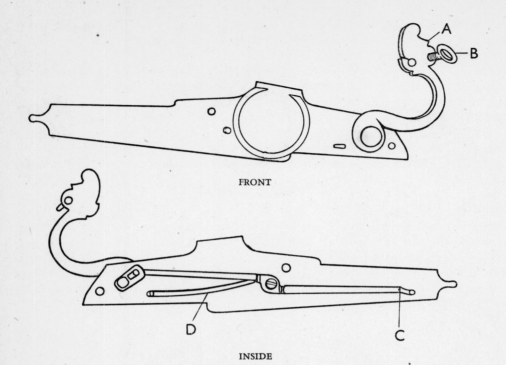

FRONT

INSIDE

Fig. 1

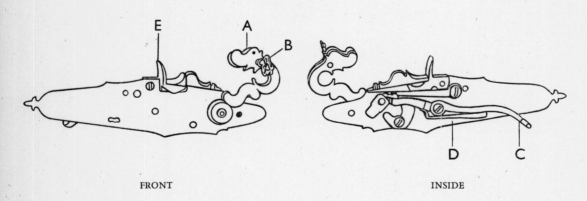

FRONT

INSIDE

Fig. 2

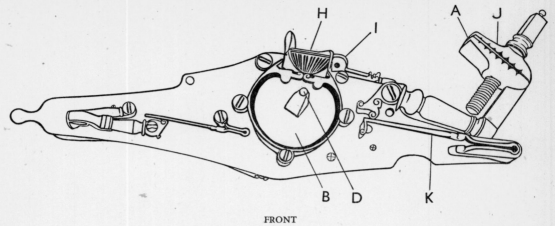

FRONT

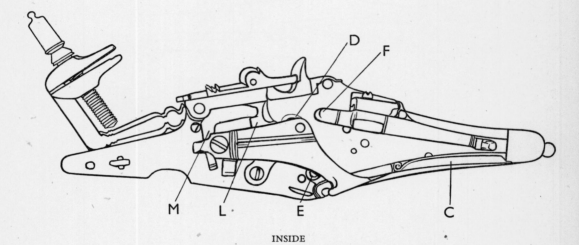

INSIDE

Fig. 3

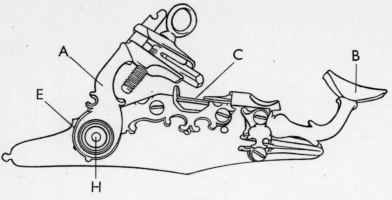

FRONT

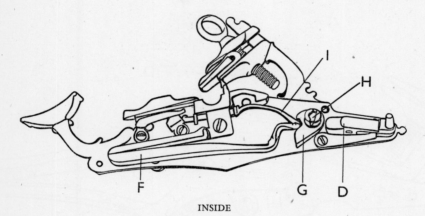

INSIDE

Fig. 4

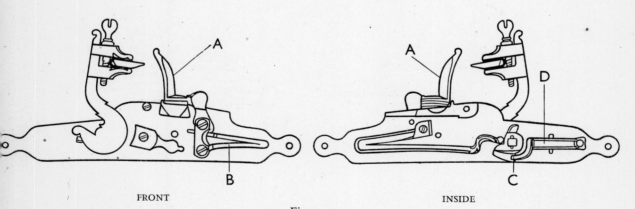

FRONT

INSIDE

Fig. 5

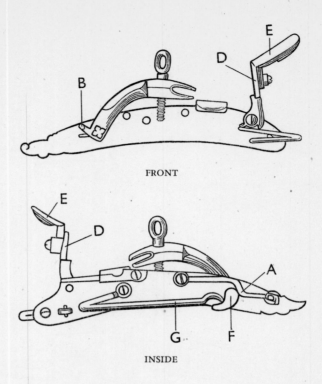

FRONT

INSIDE

Fig. 6

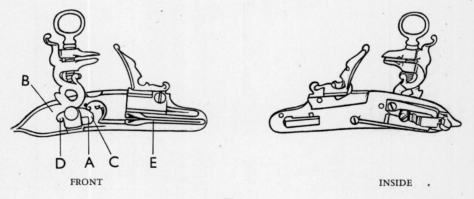

FRONT

INSIDE

Fig. 7

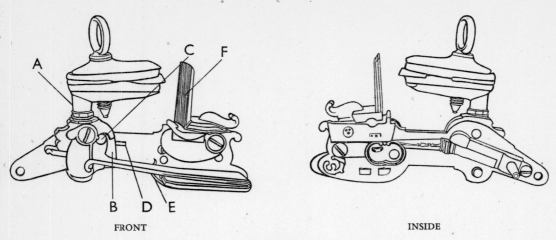

A   C   F

B   D   E

FRONT   INSIDE

Fig. 8

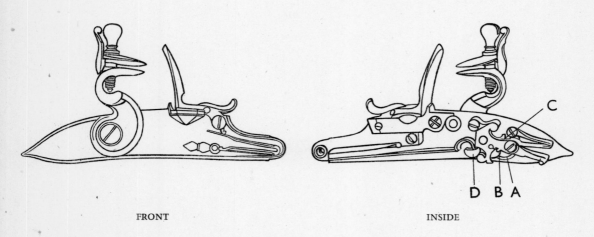

C

D   B   A

FRONT   INSIDE

Fig. 9

LIST OF ILLUSTRATIONS

1. PLATE I. WHEEL-LOCK WITH SELF-SPANNING GEAR. *South German, about* 1540. Of early type with cock-spring of circular form placed around the wheel. For convenience in spanning the cock is placed in front of rather than behind the wheel. On the lock-plate a maker's mark, a sickle (Støckel No. 5847). A similar mark, struck on the barrels of several of the wheel-lock firearms in the Madrid Armoury, is attributed to the brothers, Peter and Simon Markwart, who were brought from Augsburg to Madrid about 1530. *See* A. Hoff. 'Hjullaase med seglformet Hanefjer'. *Vaabenhist. Aarbøger*, III. p. 68. Copenhagen, 1940. *Farquharson Bequest* M.701–1927

2. PLATE II. MATCH-LOCK ARQUEBUS; the stock of walnut is profusely inlaid with 'singeries', scenes of the hunt and, on the inner side of the curved butt, with Hercules overcoming the Nemean lion. The ground is filled with foliate scrolls in engraved stag-horn, some of the leaves being stained green.

The barrel of octagonal section, at the breech a barrel-smith's mark, a star within a shaped shield. The lock of usual construction; there are traces of gilding on the lock-plate.

Probably French; second half of sixteenth century. Length 3 ft. 10 in.
Farquharson Bequest. M.485–1927

The attribution to a French rather than a Dutch or German maker is based on stylistic grounds. Such pieces were also produced in large numbers in both Germany and the Low Countries. Those stocked up in the latter region were usually provided with barrels imported from Suhl in Germany. Arquebuses of this type with hooked butt are shown in the woodcuts of Jost Amman and other contemporary artists. The inlay work on the stock with stained horn is similar to that found on contemporary French wheel-lock pistols.

A similar match-lock arquebus in the Tower of London is illustrated in Ffoullkes, Tower Armouries. Plate XXXIII (XII. 13).

3. PLATE III. WHEEL-LOCK PISTOL, the stock entirely of iron, the lock stamped with a maker's mark, a lion rampant beneath the initials H S within a shaped shield (not in Støckel). The pyrites holder engraved with a monster's head. The barrel divided into two sections, that at the breech fluted.

South German (Nürnberg?) about 1570–80. Length 29½ in. *Farquharson Bequest.*

M.631–1927

The stocks of this type of pistol were usually etched with hunting subjects and foliate scrollwork, but there is no trace of such decoration on this example. The section of the butt behind the pommel was originally bound with cord to give a better grip, but this is now missing. A similar pistol, entirely etched and gilt, is in the Wallace Collection, No. 844.

4. PLATE IV. WHEEL-LOCK REITER PISTOL, the stock inlaid with closely set spiral foliate scrolls of stag-horn enclosing grotesque masks, birds and monkeys in engraved stag-horn. The stock bears the stockmaker's signature, the initials B.H. (Støckel 2043) and the date (15)79. Large ball butt.

The lock, with exterior safety catch, is unmarked.

The barrel is lightly chiselled with grotesque masks and foliage. It bears the barrel-smith's initials and also his mark, a chamois head between the letters S R with the figures 73 in a shaped shield (Støckel 4524 and 4525). The figures should probably be read as 1573, and perhaps record the date of registration of the mark. On the barrel, the date 1579.

South German; dated 1579. Length 21 in. *From the De Cosson Coll. Christies*, May 2–3 1893. Lot 32. 612–1893

The pair to this pistol is preserved in the Musée de l'Armée, Paris (No. M1606 in the Catalogue of 1889). There are two powder flasks in the Museum decorated en suite with this pistol, though not acquired at the same time. One is circular with mounts of gilt bronze (M143–1923), the other of trefoil outline (67–1903). This pistol belongs to a large group of similarly decorated pieces, examples of which are to be seen in most of the larger public collections of

Europe. There are, or were, numbers in the Dresden Rüstkammer (*see* Haenel, *Kostbare Waffen aus der Dresdner Rüstkammer:* Tafel 74), and they are sometimes described as Saxon (e.g. Wallace Collection Catalogue. Part III No. 826), but as yet no evidence has been adduced to prove that they were made in Saxony. In general type they conform to the South German fashion of the last quarter of the sixteenth century.

5. PLATE II. WHEEL-LOCK ARQUEBUS, the walnut stock inlaid with spiral scrolls in engraved stag-horn. In the butt are receptacles for three cartridges, to which access is obtained through a trap in the butt-plate. Double wheel-lock arranged for consecutive discharge. Brass wheel-covers.

The barrel of octagonal section at the breech, the remainder round. It has two touch holes, one corresponding to each lock, providing for two charges, one loaded on top of the other. The barrel is roughly chiselled with a grotesque mask at the breech end, and with foliage at the midway point and at the muzzle. V backsight and blade foresight. The barrel is dated 1581. Maker's mark stamped on each side of the breech, an anvil over the initials N.H. (not in Stöckel).

German; dated 1581. Length 3 ft. 9 in. *Farquharson Bequest.*   M.615–1927

6. PLATE II. WHEEL-LOCK PISTOL, the walnut stock inlaid with stag-horn engraved with sea monsters and grotesque masks.

The butt-plate of brass is engraved with foliate scrolls and a coat of arms, but appears to be a later restoration. A belt-hook is attached to the stock on the opposite side to the lock; on the flattened end is a maker's mark, a hand with the letter W. (Stöckel No. 5005). The same mark appears on the belt hook of a pistol in the Berlin Zeughaus dated 1586.

The lock of usual construction with external safety catch (defective). On the lock, the Nürnberg town mark and a locksmith's mark, an owl between the letters H F in a shaped shield (not in Stöckel).

The barrel, which is swamped at the muzzle, bears the Nürnberg town mark and a barrel-smith's mark, partly obliterated.

South German (Nürnberg); last quarter of sixteenth century. Length 16 in. *Farquharson Bequest.*   M.642–1927

The presence of a belt-hook indicates that this pistol was intended to be carried by a foot soldier. Sir Martin Frobisher is shown holding a similar wheel-lock pistol in his portrait by Cornelius Ketel in the Bodleian Library, Oxford. The portrait is dated 1577.

7. PLATE III. DESIGN FOR A PAIR OF WHEEL-LOCK PISTOLS in etched outline and wash. *South German, late sixteenth century.*

E.1545

Though the designs are evidently intended for a pair of pistols, there are slight differences between the ornament of the two, mainly as regards the triggers, trigger-guards and pommels. The stocks were intended to be inlaid in engraved stag-horn, the pommels would probably have been of cast, chiselled and gilt bronze. The barrels and locks would probably have been of blued steel, chiselled against a gilt ground. The hunting scenes on the stock of the upper pistol are similar to but not identical with those in the Venationes of Jan van der Straet (1530–1605) usually known as Stradanus. The 'Grotesques' on the barrels seem to be derived from the engraved ornament of Etienne Delaune (1519–c.1588). The design and ornament of the lock is very similar to that of Daniel Sadeler of Munich (compare the lock in the Museum No. 29), and only amongst the works of the Munich school would it be possible to find existing firearms of comparable magnificence. The iron strap inset on the left-hand side of the stock opposite the lock carries a safety catch.

For a discussion of this design, see J. F. Hayward, 'A German design for a pair of wheel-lock pistols'. *Connoisseur.* Vol. CXXIII, pp. 16–18.

8. PLATE IV. PAIR OF WHEEL-LOCK REITER PISTOLS, the wood stocks overlaid with marquetry of cow-horn and stag-horn, engraved with scenes from the chase, monsters and grotesque masks. On the pommels, lion's mask medallions. The ornament is similar on each pistol.

The lock-plates bright, originally blued, the

wheel cover and springs gilt. Trigger guard and trigger gilt.

The barrels blued and gilt, chiselled with two bands of conventional foliage, and, at the breech, a grotesque mask. On the barrels, the Augsburg town mark and barrel-smith's mark of Jäger, a hunting horn (Støckel 5223).

South German (Augsburg); last quarter of sixteenth century. Length 19¼ in. *Farquharson Bequest.* M.489, 489a–1927

This is the standard type of pistol for mounted troops of the latter years of the sixteenth century. The German city arsenals used to contain them in large numbers, as does the Zeughaus of Graz in Styria still. They were carried in holsters at the saddle bow, and contemporary woodcuts show mounted men with as many as four of them. e.g. Jost Amman. *Kunstbüchlein* fol. T iii.

9–12. PLATE V. FOUR DESIGNS FOR ENGRAVED ORNAMENT ON WHEEL-LOCK RIFLE BUTT-PLATES, drawn with pen and ink and washed with colour. *German, end of the sixteenth century.* Purchased from the funds of the *Murray Bequest.* E.1990–1993

The designs belong to a series of sixty drawings, all from the same workshop; they correspond to the engraved ornament found on South German stocks of the end of the sixteenth and early seventeenth centuries. They are adapted from engravings or wood-cuts by Virgil Solis, Jost Amman and, probably, Paul Flindt. The monogram of Virgil Solis on Nos. 10 and 11 is a spurious addition. The subjects are as follows:

9. Adapted with slight alterations from the figure of a horseman on sheet T ii (obverse) of Jost Amman's *Kunstbüchlein*, published Frankfurt a. Main 1599.
10. The figures of the huntsman and the dog in the right foreground are adapted from Jost Amman's *Künstliche Wohlgerissene Figuren von allerlei Jagd-und Waidwerk,* Frankfurt a. Main, 1592, from the section headed 'Wie ein Jäger den Hirsch aufsuchen und behunden sol'. The figure of the fallen stag with the hound on the left is apparently from another wood-cut in this same work.
11. Diana with her nymphs surprised by Actaeon; in the background, Actaeon, changed into a stag, torn to pieces by his hounds.
12. Venus lamenting over the wounded Adonis. Copied with slight modification from Virgil Solis' engraving of this subject in his illustrations to Ovid's *Metamorphoses*.

The whole series of designs is fully discussed with a catalogue in *Livrustkammaren*. Stockholm. Vol. V, 7, pp. 109–34. J. F. Hayward. 'Designs for ornament on gunstocks'.

13–14. PLATE I. TWO DESIGNS FOR ENGRAVED ORNAMENT ON WHEEL-LOCK MUSKET BUTT-PLATES, drawn with pen and ink and washed with colour.

German, end of the sixteenth century. Purchased from the funds of the *Murray Bequest.* E.2002, 2003

These designs of strapwork enclosing human figures and animals recall the engraved ornament of the Nürnberg artist, Paul Flindt, who published a number of books of designs in Vienna between 1592 and 1618.

See also notes on Nos. 9–12 from the same series.

15. PLATE IV. WHEEL-LOCK PISTOL, the walnut stock, inlaid with hunting subjects amidst foliate scrollwork in engraved and partly stained stag-horn, and with plaques engraved with figures in contemporary costume in the manner of Jost Amman. Large ball butt.

The lock of French type with detached mainspring fixed separately in stock is stamped with the maker's mark, a spur (Støckel 5882). It is dated 1593 on the priming pan. Barrel of round section, the muzzle slightly swamped, stamped with the same spur mark as the barrel and with the Nürnberg town mark.

South German (Nürnberg), dated 1593. Length 1 ft. 9 in. *Joicey Bequest.* M.230–1919

This pistol is of great interest in that, though of Nürnberg manufacture, it is equipped with the typical French wheel-lock with independently attached mainspring. It constitutes an important exception to the otherwise generally valid law laid down in *Armes et Armures*. Musée de l'Armée, Vol. II, p. 117, that only French wheel-locks have this type of construction.

16. PLATE XV. DOUBLE-BARRELLED WHEEL-LOCK PETRONEL WITH TWO LOCKS, the stock inlaid with mother of pearl plaques, and with strap and scrollwork in engraved stag-horn. The stock is of an exotic wood of reddish colour; in the upper side of the butt is cut a socket into which an extra detachable butt (now missing) could be keyed. The trigger guard, ramrod pipe and the iron strap around the forestock are replacements dating from the second half of the seventeenth century.

The barrels, set side by side, are of very small bore (7 mm.). This is a normal feature of petronels of this date. The single trigger discharges the two locks consecutively.

The locks are stamped with the Nürnberg town mark and a maker's mark, a crossbow bolt over a trefoil between the letters P R. (Støckel 4347/50). This mark is recorded on barrels as well as locks, accompanied in each case by the Nürnberg town mark.

South German (Nürnberg), about 1600. Length 2 ft. 6 in.

R.U.S.I. Loan.

17. PLATE I. WHEEL-LOCK, the cock chiselled with a monster's head.

French; late sixteenth century, Stovell Bequest.
M.176–1928

The elements of this lock are all finely chiselled with details influenced by contemporary architectural ornament. For the dating of French wheel-lock firearms, *see* T. Lenk. 'De franska hjullåsvapnen' *Vaabenhistoriske Aarböger* IV. Kopenhagen, 1943.

18. PLATE XVII. WHEEL-LOCK, the surface damascened with gold and silver.

South German; about 1600.   M.402–1910

The lock-plate is engraved with two eagles with outstretched wings, enclosed within arabesques damascened in gold and silver, against a blued ground. The cock gilt.

19. PLATES VI and VII, WHEEL-LOCK RIFLE, the walnut stock inlaid with strapwork interspersed with figures in engraved stag-horn. On the cheek piece an oval medallion inlaid with figures representing Pyramus and Thisbe within a strapwork composition with figures of Putti and warriors. On the patch box cover is a figure of an officer of pikemen in costume of the early seventeenth century. The fore part of the stock inlaid with wild animals and figures amidst strapwork.

The lock, of early seventeenth century type, is engraved with a scene of Orpheus charming wild animals, the pyrites holder with the head of a monster.

The blued octagonal barrel, rifled with eight grooves, with V-backsight and blade foresight is signed at the breech H K (Støckel No. 2937 or 2944).

East German; early seventeenth century. Length 4 ft. 6½ in. *From the Shandon Collection.*
802–1877

Støckel identifies the barrel-smith H K as Saxon; but this does not necessarily mean that the stock and lock are also of Saxon origin. A detached lock in the Museum, No. M535–1924 is engraved in a similar manner. Compare also Wallace Collection No. 834; this subject seems to have been particularly popular in Eastern Germany or Poland and is frequently found engraved on the lock-plates of guns which can for other reasons be assigned to an Eastern European source.

Lit. Dr. R. Cederström 'En Danzigerbössa med Oxenstiernavapen'. *Livrustkammaren.* Vol. 3, p. 1.

20. PLATES VI, VII. WHEEL-LOCK RIFLE, the walnut stock inlaid with compositions of strapwork in engraved stag-horn. On the cheekpiece a heraldic escutcheon with the arms of Hatstein and the date 1605, within a ring inscribed MARQUARDUS VON HATSTEIN ZU WEILBACH. On a panel behind the barrel tang are engraved the initials of the stockmaker, H E.

Lock with covered wheel. To the lock-plate is attached a brass plate, formerly gilt, in the form of a sea-horse.

Octagonal barrel with V-backsight and blade foresight, rifled with eight grooves. At the breech, the barrel-smith's mark, the initials O S over a toothed wheel in a shaped shield (Støckel 4206).

German; dated 1605. Length 3 ft. 9½ in. *From the Bernal Collection.* Sale Catalogue, Lot Number 2639.   2240–1855

Weilbach is a small village to the east of Mainz on the north bank of the river Main. The arms of Hatstein are not given in the early editions of Siebmacher's *Wappenbuch*.

21. PLATES VI, VII. WHEEL-LOCK RIFLE, the stock inlaid with panels of stag-horn engraved with birds, animals and grotesques within compositions of strapwork, and with steel plaques, formerly blued, to which are applied panels of copper gilt strapwork, cast, pierced and chased. On the butt-trap cover, of stag-horn engraved with grotesques, are the initials F. F., presumably of the engraver. Iron heel plate, to which is applied a cast, chased and gilt plaque of a lady on horseback after a wood-cut by Jost Amman.

Lock of bright steel, formerly blued, to which are applied copper gilt masks and a panel of strapwork, surmounted by a female term. The wheel-cover of copper gilt, pierced and chased with tracery. The octagonal barrel, formerly blued, now bright, bears the initials G. G. of Georg Geissler (Støckel No. 434) and the date 1606. It is equipped with backsight and blade foresight, the latter a later restoration. Both are surrounded by panels of pierced and gilt scrollwork. It is rifled with eight grooves.

Saxon (Dresden); dated 1606. *Length* 4 *ft. From the Bernal Collection. Sale Catalogue, Lot* 2649.   2241–1855

Georg Gesissler, born in Strassburg, was admitted as a citizen in Dresden on 14 November 1607. He held the appointment of 'Kurfürstlicher Sächsischer Büchsenmeister'. The barrel of this rifle was evidently made before he was admitted citizen of Dresden. Støckel gives the name as 'Gessler', but W. Holzhausen, quoting the Dresden archives, gives 'Geissler' or 'Geiseler' (*Zeitschrift f. Hist. Waffenkunde*, Vol. XIV, p. 190).

22. PLATES VIII, IX. PAIR OF WHEEL-LOCK HOLSTER PISTOLS, the walnut stocks profusely inlaid with oval plaques engraved with allegorical figures within elaborate scrollwork enclosing minute human figures, animals and birds, of stag-horn and ivory. The inlaid ornament appears to be derived from engraved

designs by Theodor de Bry or Adriaen Collaett. The locks, of early seventeenth-century type, are unsigned. Octagonal barrels, the blueing renewed. Stamped at the breech, a barrel-smith's mark, partly obliterated through cleaning.

There is no feature in the mechanism or ornament which would justify an attribution to any particular locality within the German cultural area.

German; about 1600–10. *J. G. Joicey Bequest.* M.232, 232a–1919

23. PLATES VIII, IX. WHEEL-LOCK PISTOL, the ebony stock inlaid with figures in contemporary costume, amorous subjects and scenes of the chase executed in engraved mother of pearl and engraved and stained stag-horn. In the face of the stock opposite to the lock is inlaid a scene of a lady and three gentlemen at an al fresco meal accompanied by two minstrels. The engraving on the inlay work is of exceptionally fine quality. The lock, of early seventeenth-century type, has a finely chiselled pyrites holder in the form of a monster's head.

The barrel is damascened in gold and silver with panels of arabesques. The bore measures only 9 mm.

South German (Nürnberg?); first quarter of seventeenth century. Length 30½ *in. Murray Bequest.*   M.1082–1910

This pistol is one of a group of wheel-lock firearms all stocked in similar manner, that is, in ebony inlaid with mother of pearl, stag-horn and ivory stained green. Examples are to be seen in the Wallace Collection (Nos. 859, 882) in the Musée de l'Armée (Nos. M1648 and M1650). Many of the firearms in this group bear the Nürnberg town mark on the lock or barrel.

24. PLATES XI, XII. WHEEL-LOCK PISTOL, the wood stock overlaid with a casing of iron, chased with mauresque designs in which a number of Renaissance elements are introduced. The lock-plate and barrel are decorated *en suite*. The iron casing is pierced with a series of rectangular panels through which the wood of the stock may be seen. These panels are also carved with interlacing designs in

imitation of Moorish ornament. There was originally a belt-hook, but this is now missing.

The wheel-lock is dated 1614; the borders are etched with interlacing ornament.

The barrel, octagonal at the breech, is equipped with a vertical slot back-sight. There is no foresight. It is etched with mauresque panels.

Spanish (Ripoll); dated 1614. Length 22 in. From the Brett Collection; illustrated in the Catalogue. Plate C, no. 4. *Farquharson Bequest.*

M.487–1927

The form of the lock is characteristic of the productions of the Ripoll gunmakers as described by Charles Buttin in his article 'L'Arquebuserie de Ripoll', *Armes à feu et Armes Blanches*, 1914. There is however in the Museo Correr, Venice, an almost identical pistol, signed 'P. L. S. Ercole Tascha di Venezia'. A third, very similar, but with a rather stronger European element in the ornament is preserved in the Real Armeria, Madrid (Inv. No. K42). Both these pistols are illustrated by T. T. Hoopes, 'Ripollsche Radschlosspistolen'. *Zeitschrift f. Hist. Waffenkunde.* N.F. IV. pp. 226–9. The signed Venetian pistol may be the work of an emigrant from Ripoll.

25. PLATE X. LIGHT WHEEL-LOCK FOWLING-PIECE, the pearwood stock slightly carved, iron mounts. Lock of French type with detached mainspring. The barrel octagonal at the breech, the remainder round. V-backsight, stud foresight.

French; about 1620–30. Length 4 ft. From the Cabinet d'Armes of Louis XIII, King of France.

603–1864

This gun is stamped on the underside of the stock in front of the trigger-guard with the number 5 of the Inventory of the Cabinet d'Armes. The corresponding entry in the Inventory reads: 'Quarante trois arquebuses toutes simples, de 3 pieds ou environ'. In view of the extreme lightness and small size of this piece, it would appear to have been made for Louis XIII when a boy. It is not known how it reached England. It may have been taken as a trophy from the Paris Arsenal by an officer in the British Army of Occupation in Paris in 1815. Two other firearms bearing the same

Inventory number are in the Musée de l'Armée, Paris (Nos. M101, M103); another is in the Collection Pauilhac, Paris.

26. PLATE X. WHEEL-LOCK DOUBLE-BARRELLED PISTOL, the stock inlaid with foliate scrollwork and trophies of arms executed in brass wire, and set with pewter studs. The oviform pommel of wood divided into panels by strips of horn and of brass, the latter chased with running foliage, set alternately. The intervening panels inlaid with brass wire and pewter studs. The trigger-guard of iron, etched, with traces of gilding. The fore-end of brass chased with trophies of arms.

The locks of German type, the plates etched with arabesques and gilt; the moving parts of the lock blued. There is only one trigger which actuates both locks simultaneously.

The two barrels are set side by side. They are etched and gilt with interlacing strapwork forming panels enclosing trophies of arms and roses set alternately. There is no maker's mark.

French; first quarter of seventeenth century. Length 18¾ in. *From the Cabinet d'Armes of Louis XIII. A. W. Hearn Bequest.* M.13–1923

There is no trace of an inventory number on the stock of this pistol, but it corresponds exactly with the No. 237 of the Cabinet d'Armes of Louis XIII, King of France. The descriptions of this, and of the preceding piece are as follows:

236. 'Un pistolet a deux canons et deux rouets . . . les canons tout ronds et tout gravez de trophées et de roses dans des compartimens, la platine couleur d'eau montée sur un bois de poirier enrichy et tout remply de fillets de cuivre et d'estain.'

237. 'Un autre pistolet, aussy à deux rouets tout pareil au précédent, excepté que les cannons sont dorez et qu'il n'a que 18 pouces de long.'

The absence of the Inventory number can probably be explained by the fact that the stock is completely covered with inlay work which would have been damaged if a number were stamped into it.

27. PLATE X. WHEEL-LOCK ARQUEBUS, the half-length stock of pear wood, mounts of iron. The lock finely chiselled, the pyrites holder in the form of a dragon, the rear part of the lock-plate in the form of a boar's head.

The lock is constructed according to the French fashion with the mainspring set independently.

The barrel Turkish, of round section at the breech, the remainder polygonal. The point of junction of the two sections is masked by a panel of conventional foliage chiselled in the thickness of the barrel. The muzzle, of tulip shape is set with two rings of silver. Aperture rear-sight, blade foresight.

The ramrod, entirely of wood, fits loosely in its slot and is probably a restoration.

French; beginning of seventeenth century. Length 6 ft. *From the Cabinet d'Armes of Louis XIII (transferred from the Rotunda Museum, Woolwich).* M.12–1949

This is one of the firearms brought to England from Paris as trophies of war after the battle of Waterloo. Stamped in the top of the stock, immediately behind the barrel, is a segment of a circle, probably part of the number 3 of the Inventory of the Cabinet d'Armes of Louis XIII, King of France. The corresponding entry in the Inventory is 'Trente quatre arquebuses touttes simples, de 6 pieds de long ou environ'. Though the Inventory number is not clearly visible on the stock, this gun is typical of the firearms of Louis XIII, particularly as regards the stocking. In view of its provenance, the Paris Arsenal, there appears to be no reason to doubt its attribution to the personal collection of Louis XIII.

28. PLATES VIII, IX. WHEEL-LOCK PETRONEL, the walnut stock profusely inlaid with mother of pearl, stag-horn and brass wire scrolls. The mother of pearl and stag-horn plaques are roughly engraved with birds, animals and foliage. The ground between the plaques is set with silver studs and minute six-pointed stars in brass. Steel mounts, brass ramrod pipe.

Lock of French type with wheel spindle passing through the stock and pivoting in a recess cut in the side-plate. On the lock-plate a maker's mark I P over a star in a shaped shield (not in Støckel).

At the breech the barrel is ribbed; it was formerly gilt also. It is of small bore (10mm).

Northern French (Alsace?); about 1610–20. *Farquharson Bequest.* M.488–1927

Compare the similar pistol in the Wallace Collection, No. 840, Catalogue Part III, p. 347, where reference to this and other similar pieces is made. A number of pistols with stocks of this type are preserved in the *Livrustkammaren, Stockholm.* They are found with both the French and the German construction lock.

29. PLATE XII. WHEEL-LOCK, CHISELLED, GILT AND ENCRUSTED WITH GOLD from the Sadeler workshop in Munich.
South German (Munich); about 1630. *From the Magniac Collection.* 124–1897

When acquired by the Museum, this lock was mounted on the considerably later Michael Maucher rifle (124–1897). It is now exhibited separately. The arm of the cock is chiselled in the round as a dragon, the jaws of the cock as a monster's head. On the lock, chiselled in low relief is an archer killing a dragon, enclosed within foliate scrollwork. According to the system of attribution to the various masters of the Munich school, worked out by Dr. Stöcklein, this lock should be given to Emanuel Sadeler (died 1610). However, a wheel-lock pistol in the Metropolitan Museum, New York, the stock of which is entirely of iron, has a lock of very similar form, the cock formed as a dolphin, also chiselled in the round. This pistol bears the arms of Maximilian, Elector of Bavaria, a dignity which he first achieved in 1623, and must therefore be the work of Daniel Sadeler, younger brother of Emanuel. This lock should probably be attributed to him also. Dr. Stöcklein's dating of the Munich school arms is not entirely reliable. Lit. *Bulletin, Metropolitan Museum of Art,* New York. Vol. 27 (1932) pp. 16–18.

30. PLATE XI. PAIR OF WHEEL-LOCK PISTOLS, the wood stocks stained to simulate ebony. The mounts, lock-plates and barrels of brass, cast, chased and gilt. The surface of the butt is lightly incised with floral ornament, now much rubbed.

The lock-plate, of gilt brass, is finely engraved with floral scrolls, probably derived from the engraved designs of Michel le Blon. The lock is secured by three screws.

The barrel, of octagonal section at the breech

is finely engraved with flower compositions, probably derived from the *Schweiff-Büchlein* of G. Krammer of Zürich.

Swiss (Zürich); second quarter of the seventeenth century. Length 24 in. *Ramsbottom Bequest.*

M.2798, 2798a–1931

These pistols belong to a group of similar firearms, both flint-lock and wheel-lock, all with mounts of gilt and engraved brass. The group includes a wheel-lock pistol in the Metropolitan Museum, New York (illustrated and described in the Bulletin of the M.M.A., Vol. V, p. 148), signed 'Felix Werder fecit in Zürich 1630', a pair of wheel-lock pistols in the Windsor Castle Armoury Cat., No. 361 (ill. Laking, Armoury of Windsor Castle, Pl. 22), a wheel-lock pistol in the Stuyvesant Coll., U.S.A., Cat. No. 193 (ill. Bashford Dean. The Stuyvesant Collection, Pl. XLVII), signed 'Felix Weerder fecit Tiguri Anno 1640', a wheel-lock pistol from the Cabinet d'Armes of Louis XIII in the Keith Neal Coll. Warminster and a garniture of a flint-lock gun and a pair of pistols in the Vienna Waffensammlung and the Schweizerisches Landesmuseum, Zürich respectively, signed 'Felix Werder Tiguri Inventor 1652' (ill. *Flintlåset,* Pl. 32, 2, 3). Though unsigned, the pair here described can be attributed to Felix Werder also.

31. PLATE XI. PAIR OF WHEEL-LOCK PISTOLS, the walnut stocks inlaid with engraved silver plaques and silver wire scroll-work. The butt caps, fore-end and ramrod pipes of nielloed silver. The ornament on the butt caps, consisting of a blank heraldic escutcheon surrounded by foliate scrollwork enclosing trophies of arms and figures of cherubs appears to be derived from the engraved designs of Johann Theodor de Bry. The ornament inlaid in the stock on the side opposite the lock-plate, a parrot perched on a bunch of fruit, is copied from a book of engraved ornament published by Michel le Blon in Frankfurt a. Main in 1611. The relevant sheet is reproduced by Lenk, *Flintlåset,* Pl. 107, 3.

The locks, of mid-seventeenth-century type, are engraved with foliage, and show traces of gilding.

Octagonal barrels, lightly engraved with foliage; at the muzzles a chiselled moulding, originally gilt.

German (Rhineland); about 1620–30. *Length* 22¾ in. *Given from the Collection of Col. Stovell.*

M.175, 175a–1928

These pistols belong to a group, all stocked in a similar way, dating from the first half of the seventeenth century. They include the wheel-lock fowling-piece signed 'Jean Henequin à Metz 1621' in the Bayrisches National Museum, Munich (ill. *Flintlåset,* Pl. 104), the wheel-lock pistol signed by Matteus Nutten of Aachen in the National Museum Copenhagen (ill. *Flintlåset,* Pl. 105, 3), a wheel-lock carbine in the Tower of London (ex. Hearst Collection, No. XII, 1551), and another carbine in the castle of Skokloster, No. 188. With the possible exception of the fowling-piece in Munich, all these firearms, including the pistols here described, seem to have been stocked by the same hand. The only one that is signed bears the name of an Aachen maker, and it is probable that the stocker worked in the Aachen region.

32. PLATE XV. FLINT-LOCK HOLSTER PISTOL WITH TWO LOCKS FOR FIRING TWO SUPERIMPOSED CHARGES IN SUCCESSION FROM ONE BARREL.

Stock of pearwood, butt cap, fore-end and ramrod pipe (defective) of gilt copper pierced and engraved with floral ornament of a type familiar on seventeenth-century watch cases.

The barrel is cut with three slender ribs, the top one of which extends the whole length of the barrel, while the other two reach to a third of its length only. Normal flint-lock mechanism, the right-hand lock fires the first charge, the pan communicating with the forward touch-hole by means of a channel cut in a metal strap running along the side of the barrel. The locks are of early type, and have an unusual feature in the safety-catch, a stud on the outside of the lock-face which when pushed to the rear, slides a bolt into a recess cut in the spindle of the cock. The two locks are fired successively by the single trigger.

The lock-plates were formerly engraved with floral designs and gilt, *en suite* with the mounts, but only traces of this ornament are now visible.

French; about 1630–40. Length 29 in. *Transferred from the Rotunda Museum, Woolwich.*

M.8–1949

This pistol is one of a number removed from the Paris Arsenal and sent to England at the end of 1815. In view of its source, general appearance and unusual construction, it seems highly probable that it originally belonged to the Cabinet d'Armes of Louis XIII. There is, however, no trace of an inventory number on the stock, nor is it possible to identify the pistol in the fairly detailed descriptions of the Louis XIII inventory. The number stamped on the stock is that of the Woolwich Museum.

33. PLATE XIII. WHEEL-LOCK RIFLE, the walnut stock inlaid with engraved staghorn and mother of pearl. On the cheek piece an escutcheon engraved with the arms of a Prince of Liechtenstein, probably Karl Eusebius (1611–1684). The lock with external mainspring, of the usual type found with these light sporting rifles, the surface decorated with punched work, originally blued and gilt.

The octagonal barrel is rifled with eight grooves, decorated with three panels of punched foliage. These panels show traces of gilding, the remainder was formerly blued. The backsight is protected by a tube.

German; mid-seventeenth century. Length 3 ft. 9 in. *From the Bernal Collection, No* 2339.

2217–1855

These light wheel-lock rifles, said to have been used for shooting sitting birds are known as 'Tschinkes' in German. The Wallace Collection catalogue (Part III, p. 321) states that they were common in the north of Germany and the Baltic provinces. They are, however, to be found in most of the German hereditary firearms collections, and they must have been used generally in Germany. The decoration on these Tschinkes is very standardized, usually rather coarse, and it would appear that they mostly came from one, as yet unidentified, source to the east of Germany. The same type of decoration is found on some wheel-lock rifles and on flint-lock pistols and these must doubtless come from the same locality. Compare the wheel-lock rifle (M.101–1930) and the flint-lock pistol (M.33–1951) in this Museum.

The Museum collections also include a Tschinke powder flask (2246–1855).

34. PLATE XIII. WHEEL-LOCK RIFLE, the walnut stock overlaid with carved ebony, enclosing panels of carved staghorn. The whole surface is carved with interlacing strapwork interspersed with bunches of fruit and animals derived from Flemish sixteenth-century pattern books of engraved ornament, or perhaps from Jost Amman's engravings in the Flemish manner. The staghorn plaques, which are executed with exceptional fineness, are carved with hunting subjects and with half and full-length figures of Turks, including a standard bearer (on buttplate), musketeers (on underside of stock), bowmen, etc. The Turkish subjects, which reflect the endemic wars against the Turks in Eastern Europe, are probably derived from the engravings of the Nürnberg artist, Jost Amman, in particular from the series of Turkish figures in his Kunstbüchlein.

The lock, of normal German construction, is engraved over the whole of its exterior surface with figures emblematic of abundance amidst foliate scrolls. The ring securing the wheel to the lockplate and other details of the lock, the trigger and the trigger guard are gilt. A maker's mark on the lockplate is indecipherable. The octagonal barrel is engraved over its whole surface with foliate scrolls enclosing eight oval panels with emblematic female figures from muzzle to breech, as follows:

1. Temperance   2. Faith   3. Fortitude
4. Truth   5. Justice 6. Charity
7. Humility   8. Prayer

The barrel is rifled with eight grooves. There is a leaf backsight of engraved brass, blade foresight.

South German; probably Augsburg, about 1600. Length 2 ft. 8½ in.   M.48–1953

From the collection of Prince Fugger at Schloss Babenhausen, between Augsburg and Ulm. This gun was formerly exhibited in the Fugger Museum at Augsburg and was described in the catalogue of the Museum under No. 1044. 'Radschlossgewehr, (Pirschbüchse) in reicher Elfenbeinschnitzerei auf Ebenholz. Die Fläche des Radschlosses wie des Gewehrlaufes zeigt überaus reiche Gravierung. Hervorragend schöne Arbeit. 17 Jahrhundert.'

From the Fugger Collection the gun passed to the W. R. Hearst Collection, from which it was acquired for the Museum.

This gun is of unusually small proportions and may have been constructed for a young man or for a lady. The quality of the ornament of this gun is so high that there seems no reason to doubt that it was made for a member of the Fugger family. The ebony veneer is composed of a large number of small fragments pieced together; this method has presumably been adopted in order to achieve uniformity in the colour of the wood, as ebony in larger pieces has lighter streaks.

The vast majority of the German gunstocks of this period were enriched with engraved staghorn, and a carved example of this quality is most exceptional. The carving is not likely to have been executed by an ordinary gunstock-maker, but it is not possible to suggest a name for the master who was responsible for it.

35. PLATE XIV. PLATE I FROM A PATTERN BOOK OF ENGRAVED ORNAMENT FOR WHEEL-LOCK AND FLINT-LOCK FIRE-ARMS, signed 'Philippe Daubigny', containing thirteen designs on nine sheets. The first edition of Philippe Cordier Daubigny's designs was published about 1635, this plate belongs to a second edition, published by van Merlen in Paris about 1665. The date below the engraver's signature has been roughly altered from 1635 to 1665.

The designs show wheel-locks and early flint-locks, and are of considerable help in dating the early French flint-locks. The author was evidently an engraver of gun-mounts by profession. He was a member of a family of gunmakers. Lenk records two others, Isaac Cordier and Jean Cordier. Isaac is known to have worked in Fontenay and in Paris. It is probable that Philippe also worked as an engraver in Paris.

36. PLATE XIV. SHEET OF DESIGNS FOR WHEEL-LOCK FIREARMS from *Plusieurs Pieces d'Arquebuzerie Receuillies et Inventées Par François Marcou Maistre Arquebuzier à Paris*. This plate

is number three from the set of sixteen and title page. It is signed 'C. Jacquinet fec. Marcou excudit cum privil'. The first and last sheets of the set are dated 1657, in which year it was presumably published; François Marcou was a Paris gunmaker, a portrait bust of him appears on the page following the title page. He was born in 1597, and the designs seem to cover the whole of his working life as a Maitre–Arque-busier up to the year of publication. They illustrate the course of fashion for some thirty years from about 1630 or a little earlier until 1657.

37–38. PLATE XVI. TWO PRINTS FROM ENGRAVED SIDE PLATES, in the early manner of François Marcou. *French; about* 1640–50.
20125, 19057
Compare Plates 2 and 5 of Marcou's *Plusieurs Pieces d'Arquebuzerie*. These prints were made by the engraver, probably as a record of the designs he had executed.

39. PLATE XV. PRINT FROM AN EN-GRAVED GUN BARREL. Along the barrel is the legend 'Je suis à Monsieur Descourallier'. The breech of the barrel is engraved with a coat of arms, barry surmounted by a coronet. *French; second quarter of seventeenth century.* 19057

40, 41. PLATE XVI. TWO PRINTS FROM ENGRAVED FLINT-LOCK COCKS, in the manner of François Marcou. *French; about* 1640–50. E.1924, E.1919–1946
Compare Plates 5 and 9 of Marcou's *Plusieurs Pieces d'Arquebuzerie*.

42. PLATE XVI. PRINT FROM AN EN-GRAVED LOCK-PLATE, in the late manner of François Marcou. *French; mid-seventeenth century.* E.1918–1946
Compare plate 16 of Marcou's *Plusieurs Pieces d'Arquebuzerie*.

43. PLATE XVI. PRINT FROM AN EN-GRAVED SIDE-PLATE. *French; about* 1670.
E.1917–1946

44. PLATE XVII. SHEET OF DESIGNS, numbered 6, from the *Plusieurs Models des plus nouvelles manieres qui sont en usage en l'Art*

d'Arquebuserie, engraved by C. Jaquinet from firearms made by the Parisian gunmakers 'Thuraine et le Hollandois' and published in Paris about 1660.   E.1927–1946

This work was engraved by the same C. Jaquinet who signed the Marcou pattern book (No. 36). Thuraine et le Hollandois held the appointment of 'Arquebusiers Ordinaires' to the King of France. Le Hollandois was, as the name implies, of Dutch origin; his real name was Adriaen Reynier. The ornament consists of fine engraved work and shows strongly the influence of contemporary jewellers' designs.

45. PLATE XVIII. WHEEL-LOCK BELT PISTOL, the walnut stock inlaid with panels of finely-pierced and engraved steel tracery. The mounts of steel, chiselled in high relief with monsters and with floral scrollwork. The butt cap is lined with red cloth, which can be seen through the pierced tracery. There is a belt-hook. The lock has a chiselled border of flowers and fruit, the wheel is chiselled with a male term whose body develops into floral scrolls, the arm of the pyrites holder is formed as a dolphin. The barrel, octagonal at the breech, the forward part polygonal, is signed 'Lazarino Cominazzo'. The signature is much rubbed, and the spelling is therefore uncertain.

North Italian (Brescia); mid-seventeenth century. Length 16¼ in. *From the Shandon Collection. From the Gurney Collection.* Sale Catalogue 8 March 1898. Lot 260.   M.262–1923

46. PLATE XII. WHEEL-LOCK, the lock-plate overlaid with interlacing foliage in chiselled steel.

North Italian (Brescian); mid-seventeenth century. Farquharson Bequest.   M.496–1927

47. PLATE XVIII. PAIR OF SNAPHAUNCE HOLSTER PISTOLS, the walnut stocks inlaid with panels of pierced steel tracery engraved with hunting scenes within interlacing foliage. The horn fore-ends a later restoration. The mounts of pierced and chiselled steel, the pierced pommel lined with yellow silk. The locks, chiselled in high relief with monsters and foliage, are signed on the inside of the lock-plate with the initials V. F. over a pellet in a heart shield (not in Støckel). The barrels are of

octagonal section at the breech, the forward part decorated with herring-bone file-work. They are signed 'Lazarino Cominazzo'. The fine quality of these barrels suggests that they are the work of the great Brescian barrel-smith himself.

North Italian (Brescia); mid-seventeenth century. Length 21 in. *From the Bernal Collection*, Sale Catalogue, Lot No. 2671. 2242, 2242a–1855

The execution of the piercing and engraving on the steel panels inset in the stocks of these pistols is of the highest quality.

48. PLATE XX. SNAPHAUNCE LOCK, chiselled with Hercules overcoming the Nemean lion, Leda and the Swan and a Triton blowing a horn.

North Italian (Brescian); third quarter of seventeenth century.   M.362–1923

Exhibited at Ironmongers' Hall Exhibition, May 1861. Illustrated in catalogue, p.175.

49. PLATES XIX, XX. PAIR OF FLINT-LOCK HOLSTER PISTOLS, the walnut stocks slightly carved and inlaid with stag-horn scrolls. The trigger guards of steel chiselled in the form of a merman, the pommels chiselled in high relief with reclining nude figures amongst trees and flowers. Locks of Miquelet construction, the cocks chiselled in the form of a baby merman whose tail develops into a dragon's head. The lock-plates still have the characteristic profile of the wheel-lock.

The barrels, octagonal at the breech, are chiselled with longitudinal panels of foliate scrolls. The forward part of the barrel is polygonal and engraved with two bands of foliage.

Italian; mid-seventeenth century. Ramsbottom Bequest. Length 22⅝ in.   M.2800, 2800a–1931

This type of lock construction was produced in central and southern Italy. In the absence of a signature it is not possible to place it more exactly. Certain details of the carved ornament on the stocks seem to belong to a period later than the mid-seventeenth century and were probably added during the eighteenth century. For a discussion of lock constructions of this type see S. V. Grancsay 'Firearms of the Mediterranean' Parts I and II. *The American Rifleman*, February, March, 1949.

50. PLATES XIII, XIV. WHEEL-LOCK RIFLE, the pearwood stock carved and inlaid with panels of carved ivory. On the cheek-piece, an ivory plaque of Diana and Actaeon, carved in high relief, on the butt-trap cover, a composition of a female figure holding in her hands a sail (Fortuna?) supported on the back of an eagle, which holds in its claws a crown, a covered cup, a trumpet and a purse (symbolic of worldly power?). Above, a figure of cupid in flight, below three cherubs. The butt and fore part of the stock are inlaid with panels running longitudinally, carved with scenes of the chase, including figures in costume of the third quarter of the seventeenth century. The stock is signed behind the tang of the barrel 'M. M.' in monogram for Johann Michael Maucher of Schwäbisch-Gmünd.

The lock, though contemporary with the rest, is not the original. It is ornamented with finely pierced and engraved panels of flowers and foliage in brass.

The octagonal barrel is inlaid in gold with a design of lozenges at the breech. The upper plane at the breech is pierced with a vertical hole for breech loading. The hole is filled with a screw plug in which is cut a slot which serves as back-sight and at the same time gives pur-chase for a tool to unscrew it. The barrel is rifled with eight grooves.

South German (Schwäbisch-Gmünd); about 1670–80. From the Magniac Collection, Christies 4 July 1892. Lot 734. 124–1897

J. M. Maucher was born on 16 August 1645 as sixth son of the Schwäbisch-Gmünd gun-maker Georg Maucher. He worked at first in Schwäbisch-Gmünd, but moved subsequently to Würzburg, probably about 1690. He was received as a citizen of Würzburg in 1696. He is represented by a series of six wheel-lock rifles in the Bayrisches National Museum, Munich, of which the earliest is dated 1670 and is signed as having been made in Schwäbisch-Gmünd. The latest, which was made in Würz-burg, is dated 1693. These firearms are deco-rated in a similar manner to No. 50, and are described in detail by W. Boeheim. *Meister der Waffenschmiedekunst*, pp. 129–30.

Other examples are illustrated by M. v.

Ehrental. *Waffensammlung d. Fürsten Salm-Reifferscheidt.* No. 187, Pl. III, and by S. V. Grancsay. 'Carved gunstocks by Johann Michael Maucher.' *Journal of the Walters Art Gallery,* 1939. See also by the same author 'Enriched Historical Arms' *Bulletin M.M.A.,* December 1948, which describes an example acquired by the Metropolitan Museum from the Liechtenstein armoury at Vaduz.

51. PLATE XVIII. PAIR OF FLINT-LOCK HOLSTER PISTOLS, the walnut stocks inlaid with panels of pierced brass tracery engraved with snakes and dragons within floral scroll-work. The mounts of brass, pierced and chased, with the exception of the trigger-guards which are eighteenth-century replacements.

The locks, engraved with floral scrollwork, are signed Pietro Alzano, Brescia.

The barrels, of octagonal section at the breech, the forward part polygonal, are signed 'Lazarino Cominazzo'.

North Italian (Brescia); third quarter of seven-teenth century. Length 22½ in. *Farquharson Be-quest.* M.664, 664a–1927

52. PLATE XIX. PAIR OF FLINT-LOCK PISTOLS, the walnut stocks inlaid with panels of pierced steel engraved with monsters amidst foliate scrollwork. The mounts of pierced and chiselled steel; the pommel is lined with red cloth, which may be seen through the piercing.

The locks, signed Piettro Bello, are chiselled with conventional foliage.

The barrels, octagonal at the breech, are ornamented with 'herring-bone' file-work, and signed 'Bernardi Bazzone'.

North Italian (Brescia); about 1670–80. Length 15¼ in. *Ramsbottom Bequest.*

M.2799, 2799a–1931

These pistols were originally equipped with belt-hooks, now removed. Both Bello and Bazzone are recorded in Støckel as working about 1660. The Støckel entry probably re-fers to this pair of pistols.

53. PLATE XXI. PAIR OF FLINT-LOCK HOLSTER PISTOLS, with mounts of engraved and slightly chiselled iron. The stocks of burr

wood, perhaps burr walnut, terminating in horn fore-ends.

The locks engraved with trophies of arms.

The barrels, which are rifled with seven grooves, are octagonal at the breech and finely chased with foliate scrollwork enclosing naturalistically treated flowers. This ornament covers the whole of the surface of the barrels with the exception of the breech strap.

Bohemian(?); *about* 1660–80, *the barrels probably the work of Hans Keiner of Eger.* Length 20 in. *A. S. Hobson Bequest. Formerly the property of the Earl of Hyndford.*   129, 129a–1878

The stocks, locks and furniture of these pistols are very similar to English work of this period, but the fine chasing on the barrels is typical of the manner of the Sudeten-German gunsmith Hans Keiner, *see* H. Schedelmann. 'Der Büchsenschmied Hans Keiner als Meister deutschen Eisenschnitts', *Zeitschrift f. Hist. Waffenkunde.* N.F. VII, 1942, p. 149. Similar flower designs are however found on firearms made elsewhere in Germany, as for example on the lock of a wheel-lock rifle in the Tower of London signed by Andreas Prantner of Regensburg. It is not impossible that the first Earl of Hyndford (1638–1710), to whom the pistols probably belonged, had this fine pair of barrels stocked up in England. The engraved and chiselled ornament on the lock and mounts appears to be the work of a different and less skilled hand than that on the barrel.

54. PLATE XXII. FLINT-LOCK BREECH-LOADING MAGAZINE GUN, the barrel and lock signed 'John Cookson', the stock of burr walnut, the lock-plate and mounts of iron chiselled in relief and engraved with grotesque masks and monsters.

English; about 1680. Length 4 ft. 1 in.
                                                   77–1893

This type of breech-loading magazine gun is believed to have been invented by the Florentine gunmaker Michele Lorenzoni, after whom it is usually named the 'système Lorenzoni'. It was produced by gunmakers elsewhere in Europe, and it is impossible to determine to whom credit for its invention should be given.

It is to this breech-loading construction that Samuel Pepys refers in the often quoted entry in his diary of 3 July 1662, referring to 'a gun to discharge seven times, the best of all devices I ever saw, and very serviceable, and not a bawble; for it is much approved of, and many thereof made'.

The action is operated as follows. The charges of powder and ball are carried in two tubular magazines in the butt, the openings of which are closed by a revolving breech block, the axis of which is at right angles to the axis of the barrel. In the breech block are cut two chambers corresponding to the openings of the magazines. To load the piece, the breech block is revolved through half a turn by means of a lever on the left-hand side of the breech; this motion brings these two chambers into line with the magazines, and allows a bullet and a charge of powder to drop into the chambers (the weapon being held muzzle downwards during this operation). The breech block is then revolved in the reverse direction, the bullet drops into the breech end of the barrel as the bullet chamber and barrel come into line, and finally the powder chamber comes into line with the barrel, forming a temporary breech. Simultaneously the flash pan is primed with fine powder from a separate magazine acting upon the same principle as the main magazine, whilst a cam on the revolving breech block (missing on this example) thrusts back the cock into the 'half cock' position.

The John Cookson who is recorded as living in Boston, Massachusetts between 1701 and 1762 and who advertised guns of this nature for sale must have been a son of the maker of the piece discussed here. *See* R. E. Gardner, *Arms Fabricators Ancient and Modern*, Columbus, Ohio 1934, for details of the younger Cookson.

55. PLATE XIX. FLINT-LOCK PISTOL, the stock entirely of iron is signed 'Scioli in Brescia'. The surface of the stock is engraved with interlacing floral scrollwork, the mounts are chiselled with interlacing scrolls terminating in dragon's heads, the butt-cap with a bust portrait of a Roman Emperor within a laurel wreath. The lock is signed Scioli in Ba, the barrel Giovani Battista Franzino.

North Italian (Brescia); about 1680. Length 19 in. *Farquharson Bequest.*   M.490–1927

Though pistols stocked entirely in iron were usual in Germany in the sixteenth century and not unknown in the seventeenth century (Jan Cloeter of Grevenbroich), Stefano Sciolo (also spelt Sioli and Cioli) seems to have been the only Brescian gunmaker to have made iron stocks. Several are recorded, all fully signed by Scioli. A very similar pair of pistols in the Wallace Collection (Nos. 902, 907) are signed by this maker and have barrels by G. B. Francino. After those of Lazarino Cominazzo, the barrels of G. B. Francino seem to have been the most highly esteemed amongst the productions of the Brescian barrel-smiths.

For a list of other examples of firearms by these makers, *see* Wallace Coll. Cat., Part III, pp. 366 and 371. There is an unsigned pair of pistols, apparently stocked by Scioli in the Instituto de Don Juan de Valencia, Madrid, Nos. 167–8. *See* also G. M. Silverstolpe, 'An uncommon flint-lock construction during the middle of the seventeenth century'. *Livrustkammaren*, IV, 7.

56. PLATE XXVI. FLINT-LOCK PISTOL WITH THREE BARRELS, signed on the lock Lorenzoni. Burr walnut stock, the iron mounts finely chiselled with scrollwork. On the butt a faun's mask chiselled in high relief. Inlaid in the stock, behind the barrel-tang, an heraldic escutcheon chiselled with the Medici arms surmounted by the Medici Crown.

The lock-plate is engraved with a figure of a huntsman discharging a fowling-piece, and with foliate scrollwork.

The breech ends of the three barrels are enclosed by a sleeve, through which the touch hole passes. The barrels are revolved by hand; the trigger-guard operates as a locking device. When pressed upwards, it disengages from a slot cut in the sleeve and permits the barrels to revolve. The principle is that of the usual 'Wender' gun.

Italian (Florentine); about 1680. Length 11 in. *Farquharson Bequest.* M.677–1927

This pistol was made for Cosimo III, Grand Duke of Tuscany (1670–1723), or a member of his family. A fowling-piece by the London gunmaker, Dolep, in the Armeria Reale. Turin (No. T105) bears the same coat of arms on the

barrel and the initials 'F. M.' in cypher inlaid in the butt, and must therefore have belonged to Francesco Maria de Medici (1660–1710), a younger son of Cosimo III.

Michele Lorenzoni was the foremost Florentine gunmaker of his time, and a number of firearms made by him are preserved with other guns from the Medici collection in the Bargello, Florence. The magazine breech-loading system, represented in the Victoria and Albert Museum by the John Cookson gun (No. 54) is often called the 'Système Lorenzoni'. Though there are a number of Lorenzoni magazine guns made on this principle, there is no definite evidence that Lorenzoni was the first to invent it. Two guns of this type, both signed by Lorenzoni, are in the Armeria Reale, Turin (Nos. M64 and M65).

Støckel (Vol. I, p. 182) gives the dates *circa* 1695–1733 for Michele Lorenzoni, but the Dresden records show that the Kurfürst Johann Georg bought a repeating gun from him in 1684 (Seidlitz, *Die Kunst in Dresden*, Vol. IV, p. 503). The snaphaunce lock (M.546–1924) in the Museum collection is signed 'Michael Lorenzonus'.

57. PLATE XXIII. SHEET OF DESIGNS FOR ENGRAVED AND CHISELLED ORNAMENT ON FLINT-LOCK PISTOLS. Number 6 from the *Plusieurs Pieces et Ornements Darquebuzerie* engraved by Claude Simonin and published in Paris in 1685. E.3076–1910

The work consists of a title page and seven sheets of designs numbered 2 to 8. A second edition was published in 1705. As in the case of other pattern books, the designs are drawn from the works of Parisian gunmakers and represent the style which had been fashionable in Paris for about a decade prior to the date of publication. Le Languedoc, whose name appears on the barrel at the bottom of the sheet, was one of the most distinguished Parisian gunmakers of the last decades of the seventeenth century and the early decades of the eighteenth century.

58. PLATE XXIII. SHEET OF DESIGNS FOR ENGRAVED AND CHISELLED ORNAMENT ON FLINT-LOCK PISTOLS, Number 6 from the *Plusieurs Pieces et autres Ornements pour*

les Arquebusiers and engraved by Claude Simonin and his son, Jacques Simonin, and published in Paris in 1693.   E.3089–1910

This work consists of title page and ten plates numbered 2 to 11; though published eight years later, the designs in this pattern book do not differ in style from those in the earlier work. The Simonin manner can be studied on the pistols No. 56 in this catalogue and M.11–1949 in the Museum collection.

59. PLATE XXV. FLINT-LOCK PISTOL, the stock inlaid with mother of pearl and staghorn, the latter engraved with hares, hounds, a squirrel and an exotic bird.

The barrel is blued and decorated with reserved panels of punched scrollwork, these latter being gilt.

The lock is blued and damascened with flowers in silver.

East German; about 1680. Length 19 in. *Purchased from the funds of the Farquharson Bequest.*   M.33–1951

This pistol belongs to the same group as three other pieces in the Museum, the wheel-lock rifle (M.101–1930) and the wheel-lock Tschinkes (2217, 2218–1855).

60. PLATES XXVI, XXVII. PAIR OF FLINT-LOCK PISTOLS, the stocks signed 'Filippus Spinonus fecit'. The butts of brass, chased with interlacing foliage enclosing animals, birds and monsters. The stocks of walnut inlaid with steel and brass tracery engraved with foliage enclosing birds and animals in the characteristic Brescian manner. Each pistol is signed on a scroll inlaid in front of the trigger-guard; as the signature is on the stock, it would appear that Spinoni (lat. Spinonus) was a gun-stocker.

The whole surface of the locks is chiselled in high relief with foliage and with animals.

The barrels, octagonal at the breech, are engraved with floral scrolls enclosing human figures and animals.

North Italian (Brescian); late seventeenth century. Length 19½ in. *Given from the collection of Col. M. Stovell. From the Magniac Coll. Christies July 2–4, 1892, Lot 885–6.*   M.178–1928

Støckel, Vol. I, p. 289 records a Marco Spinoni as working in Italy about 1690, presumably a member of the same family as Filippo Spinoni. A very similar pair of pistols also with butts of brass, in the Real Armeria, Madrid, is signed by Antonio Venasolo in Brescia. (Nos. K.220–221).

61. PLATE XXIV. FLINT-LOCK HOLSTER PISTOL with walnut stock, the mounts slightly engraved, the side-plate pierced and chiselled with foliations. Rifled barrel, unscrewing at the breech to permit breech loading. The barrel is secured to the stock by a ring sliding on a rod; this device was necessary to free one hand when loading on horseback. The barrel stamped with the proof marks of the London Gunmakers' Company. The lock signed 'Fisher'.

English; late seventeenth century. Farquharson Bequest.   M.676–1927

The somewhat perfunctory finish of this pistol is hardly up to the usual London standard. Three gunmakers named Fisher, probably father and two sons, are recorded in the Gunmakers' Company in the third quarter of the seventeenth century.

62. PLATE XXIV. FLINT-LOCK HOLSTER PISTOL, the stock of root walnut, the mounts of steel slightly engraved, the side-plate pierced and chiselled in the form of a monster with two heads.

The barrel octagonal at the breech changing to round section, stamped with the proof mark of the London Gunmakers' Company. The lock signed 'Monlong Londini'.

English; about 1690. Length 15½ in. (the barrel has been shortened by about 2½ in.) *Given by Mr H. Furmage.*   M.554–1924

Monlong was a leading French gunmaker between about 1660 and 1680. He seems to have worked first in Angers but subsequently he went to Paris where he worked with the gunsmith, Frappier. While in partnership with Frappier, he made a series of very fine firearms for King Charles XI of Sweden. Presumably on account of the Revocation of the Edict of Nantes and the persecution of Huguenots, he came to England before 1685. According to the

Gunmakers' Company records, he was fined on February 4, 1685/6 for possession of a number of (presumably unmarked) barrels taken up in a search by the Company's wardens.

63. PLATE XXIV. FLINT-LOCK POCKET PISTOL, the stock of maple with artificially heightened figure. Octagonal barrel and box-lock, forged in one.

The lock-plate and barrel engraved with birds and foliage. Signed on the upper face of the barrel 'Wornall Londini'.

English; about 1680. *Length* 5¼ *in. Given from the collection of Col. G. Stovell.* M.185–1928

See J. F. Hayward 'English Pistols of the Seventeenth Century', *Apollo*, Vol. XLVII, p. 84.

64. PLATE XXVIII. WHEEL-LOCK RIFLE, the walnut stock carved with scrollwork in low relief and inlaid with panels of gilt brass chiselled and engraved with scrollwork. On the inner side of the trigger-guard is engraved the figure 1, indicating that this rifle was one of a pair, or part of a garniture of rifle, fowling-piece and brace of pistols. Mounts of engraved and gilt brass. Octagonal twist barrel rifled with eight grooves, inscribed in letters of silver inlaid in the breech GEORG EXL. V-backsight with folding leaves, blade foresight. Wheel-lock with internal wheel, the surface chiselled with a cavalry combat between Turkish and European troops. Trophies of Turkish arms are also engraved on the lock and on the sliding patch box cover. The lock is signed 'Christopher Jos. Frey in Minch' (München).

South German (Munich); early eighteenth century. Length 3 ft. 6 in. *From the Bernal Collection, No.* 2218. 2194–1855

The scrollwork on the stock is in the German Baroque *Knorpelwerk* style and appears to be derived from the engraved ornament of Johann Schmischek of Prague who published his *Neues Groteschgen Büchlein* about the middle of the seventeenth century. The ornament on the lock, showing battle scenes against the Turk, is typical of Bavarian and Austrian firearms of the late seventeenth and early eighteenth century. A wheel-lock in the Museum (719–1877) is engraved with a representation of the defeat of the Turks before Belgrade in 1717. It is signed 'M. Muck fec'.

65. PLATE XVII. WHEEL-LOCK, the plate chiselled with hunting scenes in low relief. Signed 'C. Öfner à Insbrug'.

Austrian (Innsbruck); early eighteenth century. Given by Mr S. J. Whawell. M.540–1924

The very fine chiselling on this lock is signed by the artist on a rock in the foreground with the monogram IMK.

66. PLATE XXV. PLATE NUMBERED 9 from the *Diverses Pieces d'Arquebuserie* engraved by Nicolas Guérard, Paris n.d. about 1700.

This work consists of ten plates including the title page. The designs are intended to be executed in chiselled steel against a gilt ground. The ornament on the stocks is intended to be inlaid in cut and engraved silver sheet or in silver wire. The engraver Nicolas Guérard was, like his predecessors in the publication of pattern books, probably an engraver of firearms mounts by profession. The text on the title page states that the engravings were executed 'Sous la conduite des plus habiles Arquebusiers de Paris'. This pattern book had considerable influence; its designs reflect the style of Bertrand Piraube, arquebusier to Louis XIV, who received *logement* in the Louvre in January, 1670. It was subsequently re-issued in a German edition by J. C. Weigel, published in Nürnberg. Amongst the pieces illustrated, numbers 68 and 75 appear to be based on Guérard. The design for silver inlay in a gun-stock shown in the illustration was repeatedly used at the Russian Imperial Armoury at Tula. A gun with stock inlaid with this design is illustrated: J. F. Hayward, 'The Imperial Russian Arms Factory of Tula', *Apollo*, August, September, 1949.

67. PLATE XXV. PAIR OF FLINT-LOCK PISTOLS, the locks signed I. Deplan à Prag. The stocks of walnut slightly carved, the mounts of ormolu chased with hunting scenes. The pommel caps are cast and chased in the form of grotesque masks. On the thumb-plate is engraved a bust figure surmounted by a crown with two female supporters.

The barrels of circular section with longitudinal sighting rib. Stamped in the Spanish manner at the breech, the signature of Jo. Deplan, above three *fleur-de-lis,* below an elephant.

The lock-plates are chiselled with hunting subjects.

Bohemian (Prague); second quarter of eighteenth century. Length 1 ft. 9¾ in.　　518, 518a–1872

According to Støckel, Johan Deplan was of Flemish origin. The Museum also possesses a flint-lock rifle (M192–1951) of similar type and provenance.

68. PLATE XXX. PAIR OF FLINT-LOCK PISTOLS, the barrels signed 'I. I. Behr'. The stocks of burr walnut, slightly carved, the mounts of bright steel, chiselled with figures of putti within panels enclosed by foliate scrolls against a gold-plated ground. On the thumb-plate and on the side-plate is chiselled a profile portrait of a man surmounted by a coronet of seven pearls.

The barrels of circular section with longitudinal sighting ribs have a silver foresight and are chiselled *en suite* with the mounts.

The locks are chiselled with foliage, figures of putti and masks against a gold plated ground.

Flemish (Liége?); first quarter of eighteenth century. Length 19¾ in. *Purchased from the funds of the Farquharson Bequest. From the Palace of Gatschina near Leningrad.*　M.184, 184a–1951

Jean Jacob Behr is believed to have been active from about 1690 till the mid-eighteenth century. He is first recorded in Würzburg but seems subsequently to have gone to the Low Countries, where he is known to have worked in Maastricht and Liége. The form of this pair of pistols and, in particular, the design and execution of the chiselling suggest a Liége origin. A pistol with ornament apparently chiselled by the same hand in the author's collection is signed 'Devillers a Liége'.

69. PLATE XXV. PAIR OF FLINT-LOCK CANNON-BARRELLED PISTOLS, the stocks of silver, the butts decorated with grotesque masks, the remainder engraved with late Baroque scrollwork. The thumb-plate escutcheon is engraved with the arms of the Counts Bethlen de Bethlen in Hungary: azure, a snake crowned, holding an orb between its teeth.

The cannon barrels are rifled with seven grooves; there are no sights. The ramrod is of steel, the top fits into a ramrod pipe screwed to the underside of the barrel in front of the trigger-guard.

The locks are signed 'Devillers à Liége'.

Flemish; about 1720–30. Length 15½ in. *Purchased from the funds of the Farquharson Bequest.*
　　　　　　　　　　　　　　　　M.196–1951

Unlike the usual English type of cannon-barrelled pistol, these examples have fixed barrels and must be loaded from the muzzle. In other respects, however, they follow the English pattern of the early eighteenth century, and were most probably modelled on an English prototype. At the time that these pistols were made, Liége was part of the Austrian Netherlands, and it is not therefore surprising to find a Hungarian Count purchasing firearms there.

70. PLATE XXIV. FLINT-LOCK SCREW-BARRELLED PISTOL, the lock signed W. TUR-VEY, LONDON, the walnut stock slightly carved, mounted with silver and inlaid with silver wire filigree. The barrel of 'cannon' form unscrews at the breech to allow the charge to be inserted directly into the chamber.

English (London); about 1725–30. Length 11¼ in. *Given by Mr H. Furmago.*　M.555–1924

These pistols are commonly referred to as of 'Queen Anne cannon-barrelled type', but this term is of recent introduction. They are believed to have been referred to as 'turn off' pistols at the time. The great majority date from after the death of Queen Anne in 1714. The sparse silver wire inlay on this pistol dates it fairly early in the eighteenth century. Subsequently the inlay became much more profuse. Members of the Turvey family are recorded as gunmakers during the late seventeenth century and first half of the eighteenth century. W. Turvey, the maker of this example, was probably the son of E. Turvey who was at work *circa.* 1700. Lit. J. F. Hayward 'English Screw-barrelled pistols, 1700–1750.' *Apollo,* Vol. XL, p. 114.

71. PLATE XXVII. SHEET OF DESIGNS FOR ENGRAVED AND CHISELLED ORNA-MENT ON FLINT-LOCK FIREARMS, from the

Nouveaux desseins d'Arquebuseries, engraved by De Lacollombe and published in Paris in 1730. The sheet illustrated is signed 'De Lacollombe Fecit'. E.212–1927

Sheet numbered 4 (at a later date) from a set of twelve with title page, consisting partly of the work of De Lacollombe and partly of the work of Gilles Demarteau, *see also* 72.

72. PLATE XXXIII. SHEET OF DESIGNS FOR CHISELLED AND CARVED ORNAMENT ON FLINT-LOCK FIREARMS, signed 'De Marteau Fecit' and dated 1749. E.219–1927

De Marteau seems to have added a number of plates at various later dates to the De Lacollombe set, which was published in 1730. His designs shew the full effect of the French Rocaille fashion, while the sheets signed by De Lacollombe are still in the French Régence style.

73. PLATES XXVIII, XXIX. FLINT-LOCK FOWLING-PIECE, the walnut stock of half length, carved with shells and foliate scrolls. Silver mounts, chased and engraved with strap-work and classical bust figures, in the manner of the engraved designs of De Lacollombe, published in Paris about 1700. On the thumb plate, the arms of Saxony, surmounted by a Grand-ducal crown.

The lock engraved with the figure of a huntsman in contemporary dress and with foliate scrolls. Signed 'Tanner à Gotha. 1724'.
Octagonal barrel of watered (Damascus) steel, the surface etched to bring up the pattern.
German (Gotha); dated 1724. *Purchased from the funds of the Farquharson Bequest. From the Gewehrkammer of the Grand-duke Ernst August of Saxe Weimar.* M.65–1950

In view of the Saxon arms on the thumb plate, this gun must have been made specially for the use of the Grand-duke Ernst August of Saxe Weimar. It was preserved until 1927 in the very extensive Saxe Weimar *Gewehrkammer* in Schloss Ettersburg in Saxony. Peter Tanner of Gotha (1666–1750) was a gunmaker of considerable note and firearms signed by him are to be found in most of the larger collections of firearms formed in Europe during the eighteenth century. He held the office of

fürstlicher Hofbüchsenmacher to the Dukes of Saxe-Coburg-Gotha.

74. PLATES XXVI, XXVII. FLINT-LOCK FOWLING-PIECE, the half-length walnut stock slightly carved. The mounts are, with the exception of the butt-plate and thumb-plate which are of silver parcel gilt, of gilt brass encrusted with finely-chased panels of silver. The ornament consists of classical busts chased in high relief in silver, surrounded by panels of silver, chased with arabesque designs against a punched ground, and inset in the gilt frame of the mounts.

The lock of usual construction, is signed C. Galavrino. It is finely chiselled with arabesques enclosing animals and monsters.

The barrel of octagonal section at the breech is inlaid with chased silver panels and with brass strapwork against a brown ground. The remainder of the barrel of circular section. Chased silver foresight.
South or Central Italian; second quarter of the eighteenth century. Length 5 ft. 7 in. *Given by Mr W. Russell.* M.43–1938

75. PLATE XXX. FLINT-LOCK PISTOL, the stock of burr wood slightly carved to outline the mounts.

The mounts of iron chiselled with foliage and gilt; the ramrod of iron damascened with gold is of Indian origin and has been added at a later date.

The lock-plate is chiselled with foliage and gilt *en suite* with the mounts. Underneath the cock, stamped in the lock-plate with single letter punches, the inscription REGGYA. ARMERYA. DY. TORYNO.

The barrel, octagonal at the breech, the remainder round, is blued. In the upper plane of the barrel are inset two stamps of copper, cased with gold foil. One bears the crowned arms of Savoy, the other a bull rampant, the device of the city of Turin.
North Italian (Turin); second quarter of eighteenth century. Length 20½ in. *Ramsbottom Bequest.* M.2817–1931

This pistol was made in the Royal Armoury of the Kings of Sardinia at Turin. This armoury was probably mainly concerned with the production of military arms but evidently also made firearms for the personal use of the King. It was probably made during the reign of Vittorio Amadeo II, who abdicated in 1730.

Illustrated and described, J. F. Hayward; *Bolletino Piemontese d'Archeologia e di Belle Arti*, 1949, p. 162. 'A flint-lock pistol from Turin.'

76. PLATES XXXI, XXXII. FLINT-LOCK FOWLING-PIECE, the barrel signed 'Wilson, London', the mounts of silver bear the London hall-mark for 1749–50 and the maker's mark of Jeremiah Ashley.

The walnut stock is inlaid with trophies of arms enclosed with fine rococo scrollwork executed in silver wire. The silver mounts are cast and chased with trophies of arms. The silversmith's mark is struck on the trigger-guard and on the butt-plate.

The lock is chiselled with panels containing trophies of arms against a matted gilt ground. It is signed 'Wilson'.

The barrel of round section is decorated with a panel of chiselled ornament against a matted gilt ground at the breech, and with damascened scrollwork around the fore-sight. It is signed at the breech 'Wilson London'. At the side of the breech, the London Gunmaker's proof and the maker's mark of R. Wilson.

English (London); 1749–50. Length 4 ft. 5 in.
8–1883

Wilson seems to have produced a considerable number of richly-decorated arms, many of them, to judge from their ornament, intended for export to the Near East. He was one of the few London gunmakers who practised the technique of chiselling against a gilt ground.

77. PLATES XXVIII, XXIX. FLINT-LOCK FOWLING-PIECE, the carved walnut stock inset with plaques of iron, chiselled and gilt, and inlaid with silver wire. The mounts of iron, finely chiselled and gilt, the side-plate with hounds within a landscape, the butt-strap with stags in a forest, and the butt-plate with a fallen stag amongst hounds. On the thumb-plate escutcheon is chiselled a male bust, perhaps the owner. On the tang of the ramrod pipe, a female bust, perhaps a portrait of the owner's spouse.

The lock-plate chiselled and gilt with deer and a landscape enclosed within rococo scroll borders.

The barrel of circular section, with a longitudinal sighting rib along the top; at the breech, a panel chiselled with a gentleman in mid-eighteenth-century costume carrying a fowling-piece accompanied by a dog within a garden background with a temple. At the muzzle a composition of asymmetrical scrollwork.

German (Thuringia); about 1750. This gun was formerly in the Figdor Collection, whence it passed to the Oesterreichisches Museum, Vienna. It was exchanged out of the Oesterreichisches Museum in 1935. Purchased under the bequest of Major V. A. Farquharson. M.54–1949

Though this gun is unsigned, the design of the ornament and the excellent quality of the chiselling point quite certainly to the Stockmar workshop at Heidersbach near Suhl in Thuringia. This workshop consisted of the father, Johann Nikolaus Stockmar, his two sons, Johann Christoph and Johann Wolf Heinrich and a fourth member, Johann Georg, whose precise relationship to the others has not been established. The father and both sons were appointed *Kurfürstlicher Hofgraveur*, a position which the father held from 1731 to 1745. Although they were called engravers, they were, in fact, gunmakers to the Saxon court, and most of the fine arms made by them were intended for the Elector's own use, for members of his court, or as gifts to foreign princes. They were usually made in sets of a brace of pistols, a fowling-piece and a rifle. Two complete sets exist in England, one in the Wallace Collection (Nos. 924–5, 1356, 1362), the other in the Royal Collection at Windsor Castle (Nos. 485–6, 423, 405). In each case the rifle only is signed, the Wallace Collection example by J. C. Stockmar and that in Windsor Castle by J. G. Weiss, presumably a craftsman in the Stockmar workshop. All the recorded Stockmar guns belong to the same period, about 1730 to 1760, and show the most flamboyant rococo taste. Illustrated and described, *Connoisseur*, Vol. CXXIV. No. 514, p. 128 ff.

78. PLATES XXXI, XXXII, XXXIII. AIR-GUN, the walnut stock finely carved with foliage and with rococo scrollwork, and inlaid with panels of chased or engraved silver. The remaining surface of the stock inlaid with silver wire scrollwork within which are inlaid naturalistic flowers, executed in cut and engraved silver. The silver panels inlaid in the stock represent, on the left-hand side, a figure of Minerva (or perhaps Britannia) surrounded by trophies of arms and of abundance, above her flies Mercury; on the right-hand side, a lion and an eagle, the latter symbolizing Jupiter. The panels on the forestock are engraved with cherubs and trophies of arms. In the butt-plate is a silver trap which, when opened, gives access to the pump. This operates in a cylindrical cavity bored through the butt. The mounts of silver are finely chased; the side-plate is pierced and chased with a seated figure of a winged divinity with two cherubs symbolic of the winds surrounded by military trophies.

The trigger-guard is chased with a recumbent lion under a baldachin supported by a male and a female term, and, on the loop, with a figure of Minerva (or Britannia) accompanied by trophies of arms within rococo scrolls, the thumb-plate with a putti and military trophies, the butt-plate with a scene of citizens handing over the keys of a city, in the background, combating warriors. The two upper ramrod pipes are later and inferior restorations. The lock is chiselled against a granulated gilt ground, the cock with Jupiter brandishing the Fulmen, the plate with scrollwork and military trophies. It is signed Kolbe. The lock is of normal flint-lock construction; when the scear is released, the tumbler turns and forces down a lever which in turn opens the valve of the compressed air cylinder.

The barrel of brass is covered at the breech by a sleeve of silver; this is chased with a figure of Mars amongst trophies of arms. The barrel is signed 'Kolbe Fecit Londini'. The actual barrel is contained within a brass cylinder which serves as the compressed air container. There is a back-sight and a fore-sight, the latter formed as a grotesque mask.

English (London); about 1735–40. Length 4 ft. 5½ in. *From the collection of Alexander Davison, sold St. James Square,* 21 April 1817. Lot 592.   494–1894

When sold in 1817, this gun was described as having been 'formerly in the possession of George II'. Though it is not possible to prove this assertion, the piece is of such splendid quality that it must have been made for some very influential personage. If it was made for the King, it is surprising that the escutcheon should have been left blank.

Johann Gottfried Kolb (or Kolbe) was an iron-chiseller and engraver of Suhl in Thuringia. According to Støckel, Kolb was active in Suhl from about 1735 to 1753, but the gunmakers' company minutes show that he was in London from 1730–7. An air-gun of similar construction signed by him is in the Keith Neal Collection, Warminster, and there is a pair of five-barrelled pistols signed 'Kolbe Invt London' in the Windsor Armoury (Nos. 798, 807). Lit. J. F. Hayward, 'Fine English Firearms of the period 1680–1780'. *Apollo,* February 1946.

79. PLATES XXIX, XXX. PAIR OF FLINT-LOCK HOLSTER PISTOLS, the locks signed 'Les La Roche aux Galleries du Louvre'.

The walnut stocks are slightly carved with scrollwork and profusely inlaid with symmetrically arranged scrollwork in gold wire. On the upper side of the butt is inlaid on the one pistol, a *fleur-de-lis,* and on the other, the cypher of Louis XV, King of France. The escutcheon plates of gold bear the royal arms of France.

The steel mounts are chiselled in unusually high relief against a gold-plated ground, the ornament differing on each pistol. No. 1 on pommel, (*a*) Apollo, (*b*) Jason with the golden fleece, (*c*) (on pommel cap) Prometheus bound to a rock. No. 2, (*a*) Achilles and Patroclus, (*b*) Medea killing her children, (*c*) (on pommel cap) Milo devoured by wolves.

The locks are chiselled in high relief with figure subjects against a gold plated ground, as follows:

No. 1. Medea brewing poison, and (on pancover) Diana with Cupid. No. 2. Amphitrite, and (on pancover) Neptune.

On each of the cock screws is chiselled a

profile head of Louis XV. The barrels are chiselled at the breech end against a gold-plated ground with (No. 1) Hercules overcoming Antaeus and (No. 2) Hercules slaying the monster *Geryones*. The remaining section of the barrel is blued and heavily encrusted with gold, chiselled with figures emblematic of fame and the martial virtues.

French (Paris); about 1750–60. *Length* 19½ in. *From the Bernal Collection.* Lot 2675.

2243, 2243a–1855

In view of the presence of the French royal arms on the escutcheon, the cypher of Louis XV inlaid in the stock, and his portrait on the lock, it would appear that these pistols were made for the personal use of Louis XV, King of France (1715–1774).

Jean Baptiste La Roche was Arquebusier du Roi and was granted *logement* in the Louvre in 1743; he died in 1769. The signature Les La Roche was used by J. B. La Roche in his later life when he was assisted by his son. Compare the pistol in the Wallace Collection (No. 918) believed to have been made for Louis, Dauphin of France.

An almost identical but slightly earlier pair by the same maker is preserved in the Palace of Capodimonte, Naples. These retain their original case, covered with red morocco and lined with blue silk. On the case is the monogram of Prince Ferdinand as used before his accession to the throne as King of the Two Sicilies in 1759. They were presumably a gift from Louis XV.

A flint-lock fowling-piece in the Bayrisches National Museum, Munich (No. w2890), decorated almost *en suite* with this pair of pistols and evidently by the same hand, is signed 'Arault à Versailles'.

La Roche seems to have specialized in the production of highly-decorated guns, most of which were doubtless intended for presentation by the French King to foreign potentates.

Literature T. Lenk, *Flintlåset*, pp. 113–15; several of La Roche's works are illustrated in Plates 92, 93. Wallace Collection Catalogue, *Arms and Armour*, Part III (No. 918), gives a list of firearms signed by this maker.

80. PLATE XXXI. FLINT-LOCK FOWLING PIECE, the walnut stock of half-length slightly carved, the mounts of silver, chased with hunting subjects and with trophies. On the butt-plate, the Paris hall-mark for 1777–8. The comb of the butt is provided with a green velvet cheek-piece.

The lock-plate, chiselled and gilt with a reclining huntsman with hound, is signed 'Delety à Paris Rue Coquilliere'.

The barrel, octagonal at the breech, is of round section towards the muzzle and is provided with a sighting rib along the top. The barrel is blued and gilt, the section towards the breech is incised with foliage and trophies. It bears the stamp of A. P. Esteva of Barcelona (Støckel No. 328).

French (Paris); dated 1777–8. *Length* 4 ft. 7 in. *From the Bernal Collection. Lot* 2219. 2195–1855.

This gun was constructed for firing from the left shoulder; the lock is placed on the left-hand side of the stock. Støckel records two masters of this name, presumably father and son, working in the rue Coquillière, Paris.

81. PLATE XXXIV. PAIR OF DOUBLE-BARRELLED FLINT-LOCK POCKET PISTOLS, walnut stocks with chequered grips, the engraved silver mounts bear the London hall-mark for 1823–4. Octagonal blued barrels arranged one over the other, the signature J. EGG LONDON inlaid in gold lettering. Pommel caps of gold, engraved with a cypher (owner's initials). The locks are fitted with external mainsprings linked to the toe of the cock and are signed Josh. Egg.

English; dated 1823. *Length* 6⅛ in. *Ramsbottom Bequest.* M.2802a–1931

With their waterproof pans and spurred cocks, these pistols represent the last development of the flint-lock in England. The mainspring acts on both the cock and the frizzen and is a version of the earlier Spanish Miquelet lock. The single trigger discharges the two barrels consecutively.

Joseph Egg, son of the famous maker of duelling pistols, Durs Egg, was in business at No. 4, Piccadilly.

THE PLATES

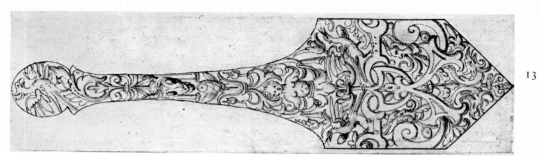

13

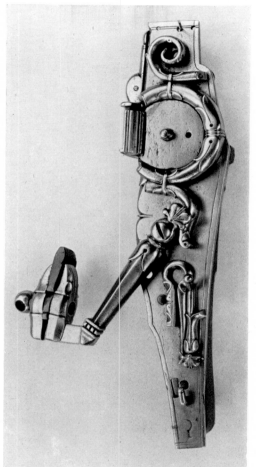

I

17

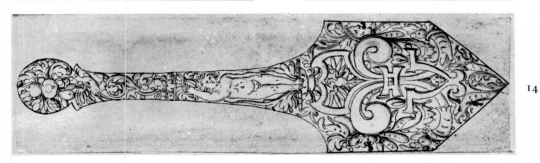

14

PLATE I: 13, 14, designs for engraved ornament on butt-plates, German, late sixteenth century; 1, 17,
wheel-locks, German, about 1540; French, late sixteenth century.

PLATE II: 2, match-lock arquebus, French; 6, 5, wheel-lock pistol and gun with double lock for super-imposed load, German, second half of sixteenth century.

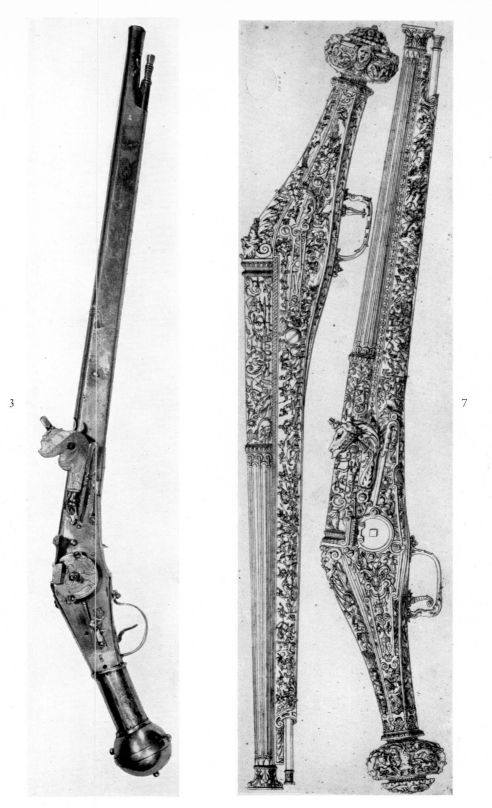

PLATE III: 3, wheel-lock petronel; 7, design for pair of wheel-lock pistols, German, last quarter of
sixteenth century.

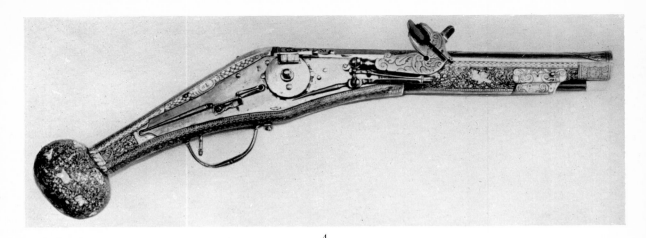

4

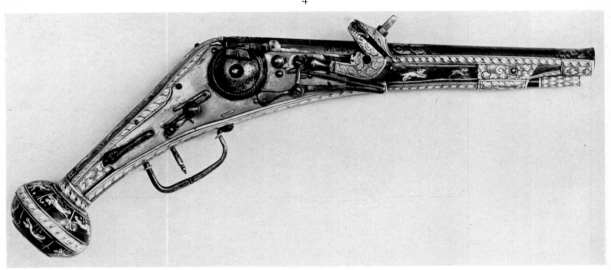

8

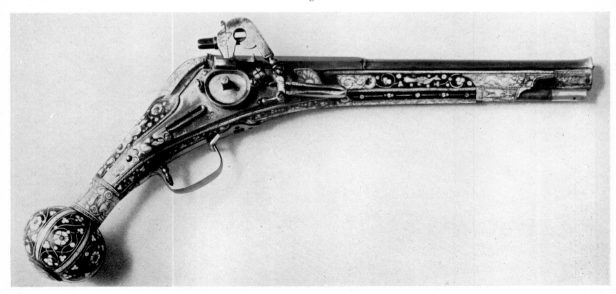

15

PLATE IV: Wheel-lock pistols, German, late sixteenth century.

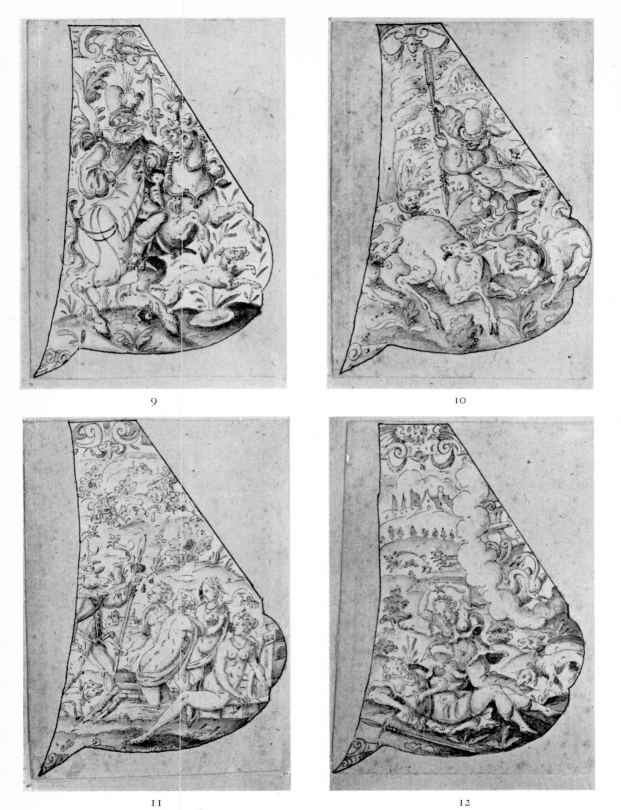

9   10

11   12

PLATE V: Designs for engraved ornament on butt-plates, German, late sixteenth century.

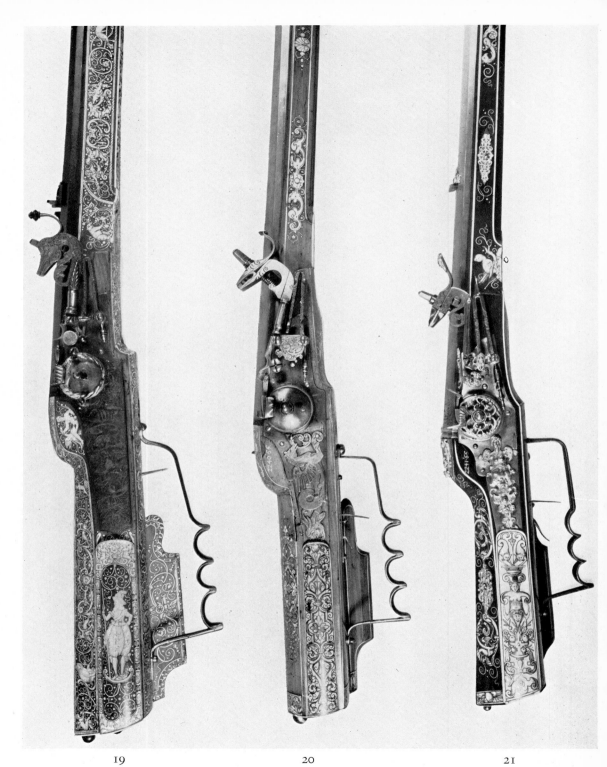

19   20   21

PLATE VI: Wheel-lock rifles, German, early seventeenth century.

19

20

21

PLATE VII: Details of rifles on PLATE VI.

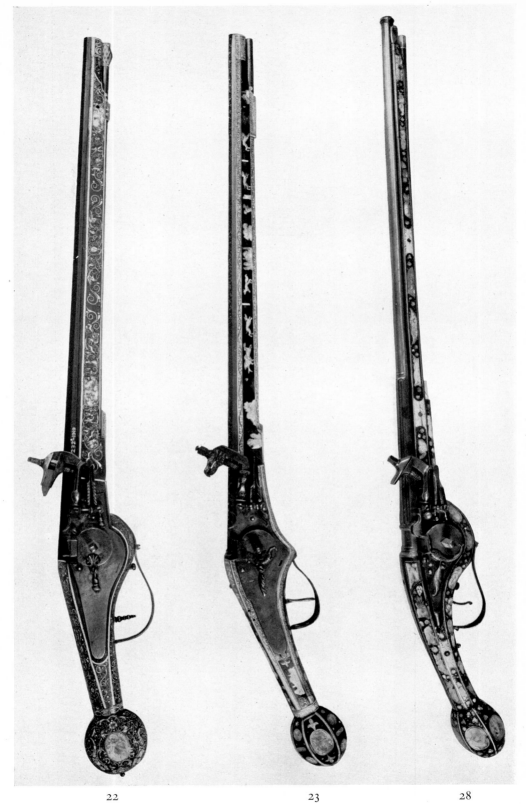

22   23   28

PLATE VIII: Wheel-lock pistols, German and French, early seventeenth century.

22

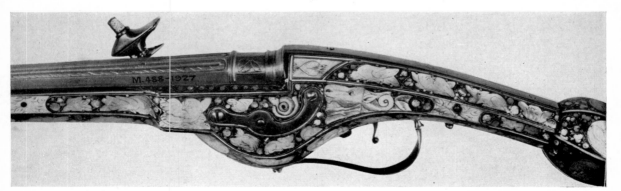

23

28

PLATE IX: Details of pistols on PLATE VIII.

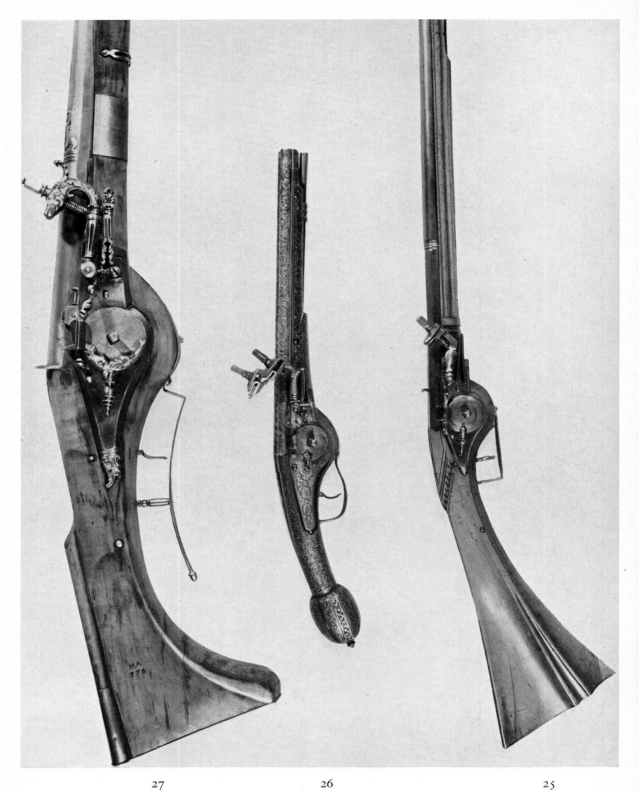

27   26   25

PLATE X: Wheel-lock firearms, French, first quarter of seventeenth century.

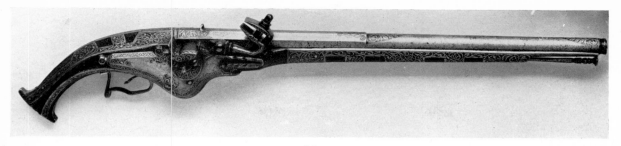

24

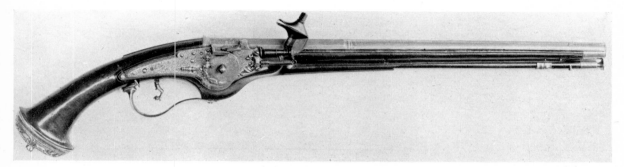

30

31

31

PLATE XI: Wheel-lock pistols, first half of seventeenth century; 24, Spanish; 30, Swiss; 31, German (Rhineland).

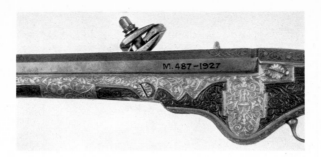

24

29

29

46

PLATE XII: 24, detail of pistol on PLATE XI; 29, 46, wheel-locks, second quarter of seventeenth century.

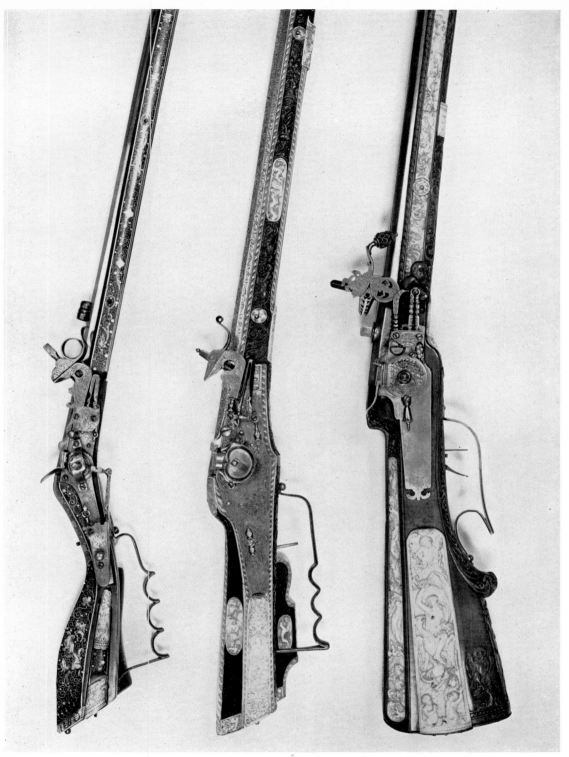

PLATE XIII: Wheel-lock rifles, German, seventeenth century.

50

35

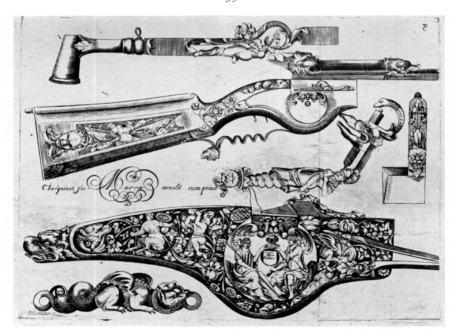

36

PLATE XIV: 50, detail of rifle on PLATE XIII; 35, 36, designs from French mid-seventeenth century pattern books.

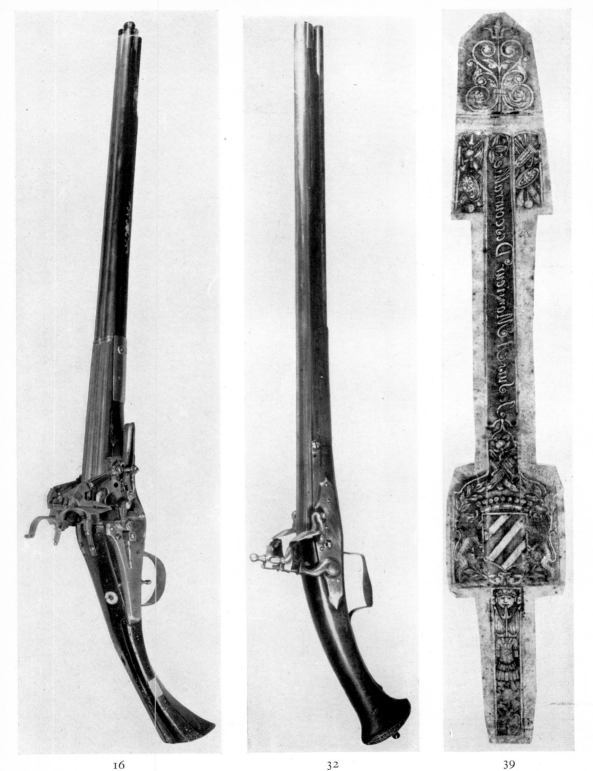

16   32   39

PLATE XV: 16, German double-barrelled wheel-lock pistol; 32, French flint-lock pistol firing two charges from a single barrel; 39, print from ornament on French gun-barrel.

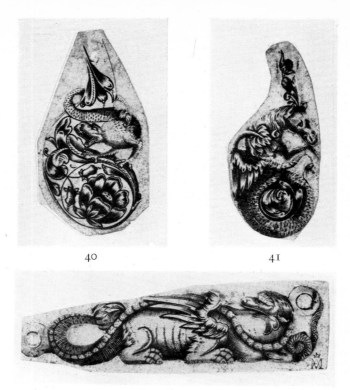

40

41

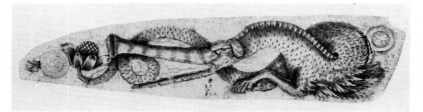

37

38

42

43

PLATE XVI: Prints from engraved ornament on French mid-seventeenth century firearms.

44

65

18

PLATE XVII: 44, engraved sheet from French mid-seventeenth century pattern book; 65, 18, wheel-locks, German, early eighteenth and early seventeenth century.

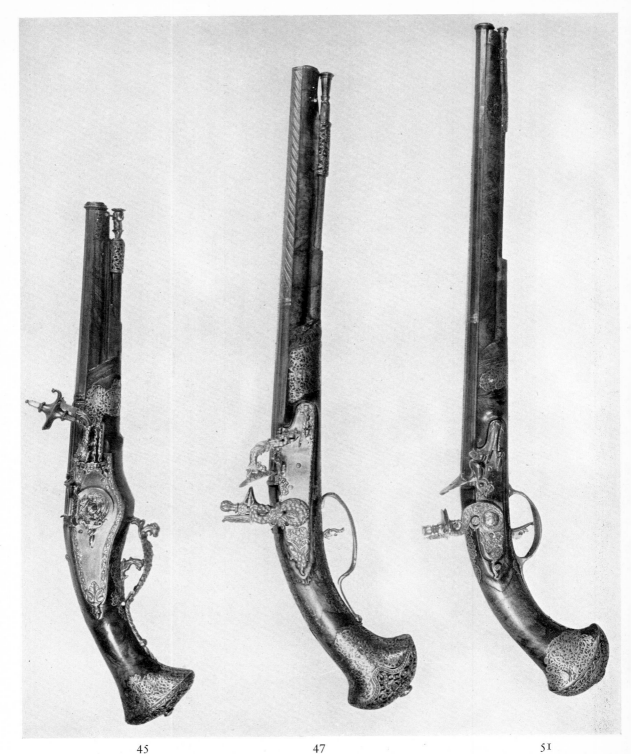

45   47   51

PLATE XVIII: Brescian pistols, mid– and second half of seventeenth century.

55

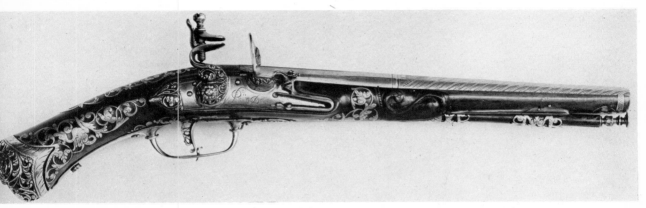

52

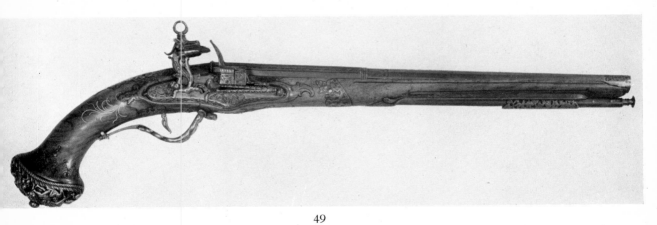

49

PLATE XIX: Italian flint-lock pistols, second half of seventeenth century.

48

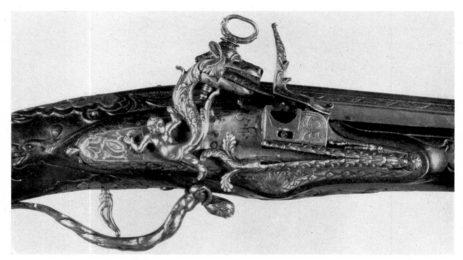

49

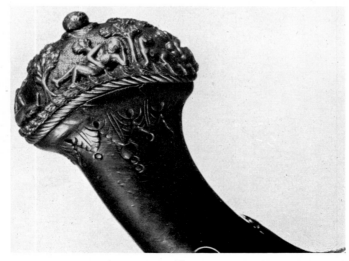

49

PLATE XX: Details of Italian steel chiselling, second half of seventeenth century.

53
53

PLATE XXI: Pair of flint-lock pistols, Bohemian, third quarter of seventeenth century.

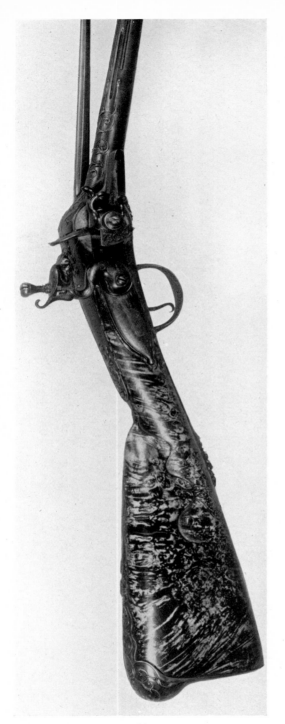

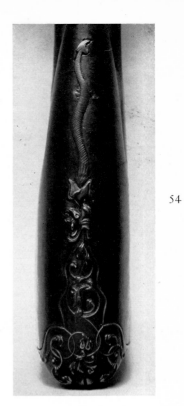

54

PLATE XXII: Breech-loading repeating gun, English, about 1680.

57

58

PLATE XXIII: Two sheets from French pattern books of late seventeenth century.

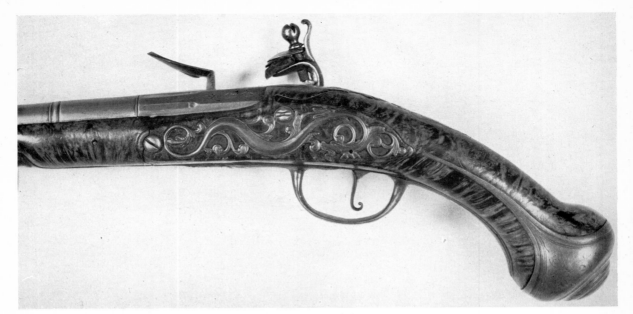

62

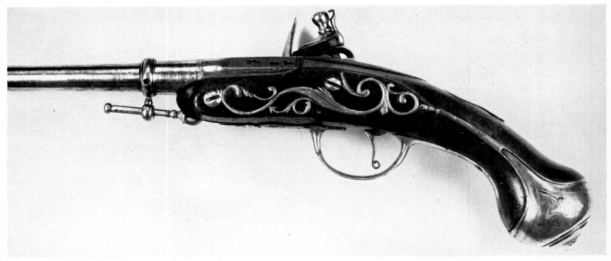

61

63   70

PLATE XXIV: English flint-lock pistols of late seventeenth and early eighteenth century.

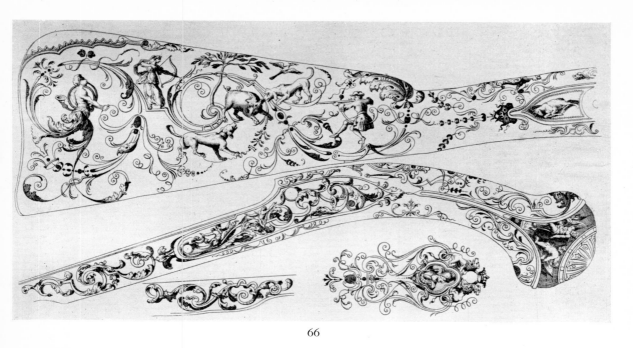

66

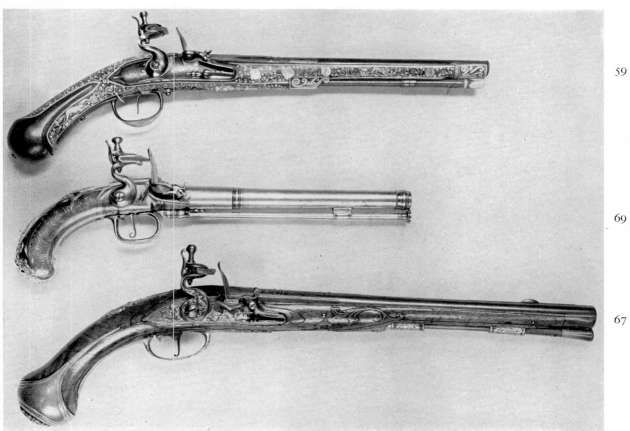

59

69

67

PLATE XXV: 66, sheet from French pattern book of about 1700; 59, 69, 67, flint-lock pistols of late seventeenth and early eighteenth century.

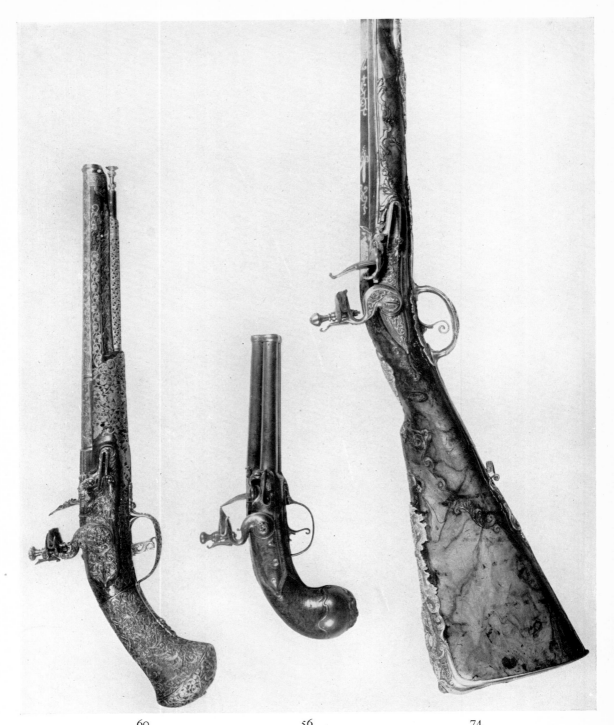

60   56   74

PLATE XXVI: Italian flint-lock firearms of late seventeenth and eighteenth centuries.

71

74

60

PLATE XXVII: 71, sheet of designs from French pattern book of 1730; 74, 60, details of flint-lock firearms
ON PLATE XXVI.

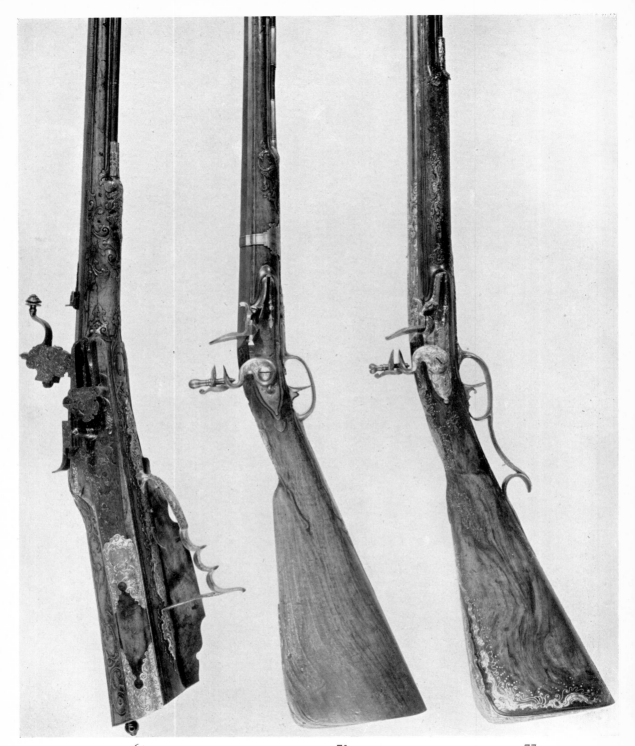

64   73   77

PLATE XXVIII: German wheel-lock and flint-lock firearms of first half of eighteenth century.

73

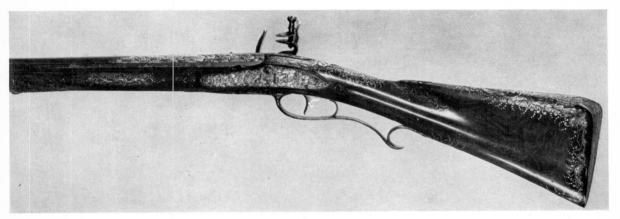

77

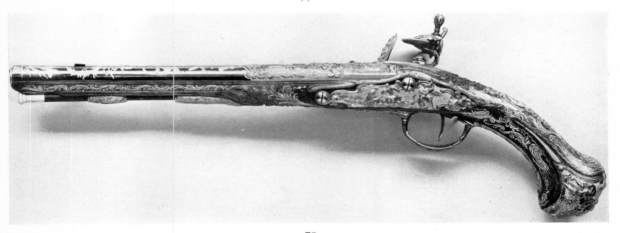

79

PLATE XXIX: German and French flint-lock firearms of eighteenth century.

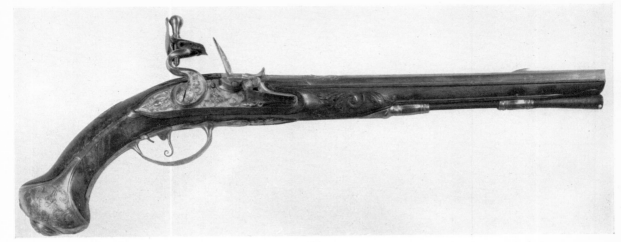

68

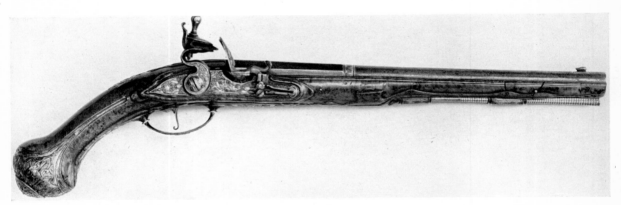

75

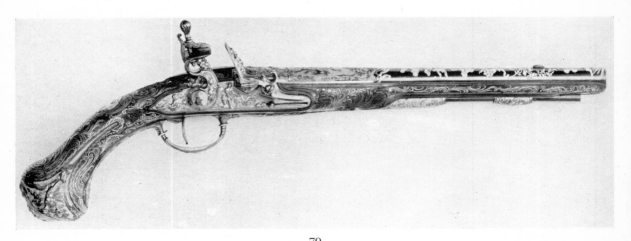

79

PLATE XXX: Flint-lock pistols of first half of eighteenth century.

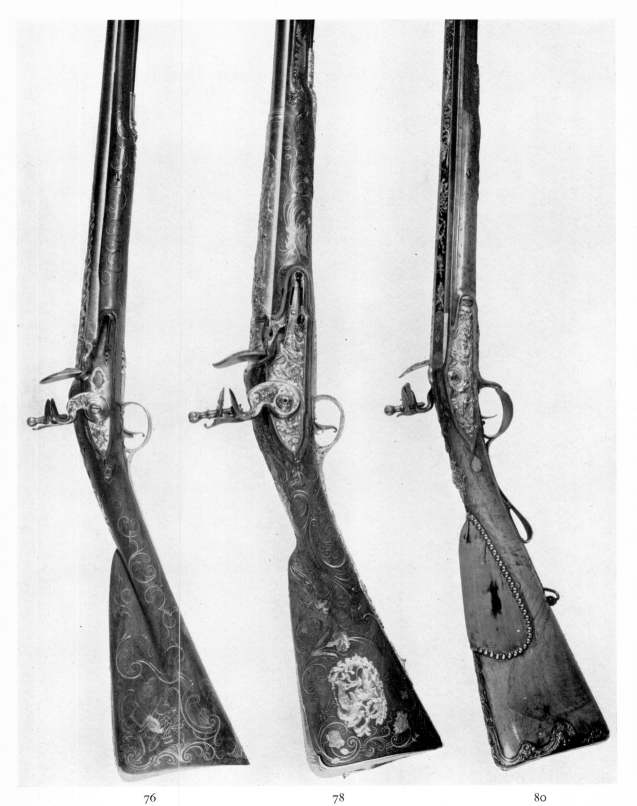

PLATE XXXI: Air gun (78) and two flint-lock guns of mid- and second half of eighteenth century.

78

78

76

PLATE XXXII: Details of firearms on PLATE XXXI.

72

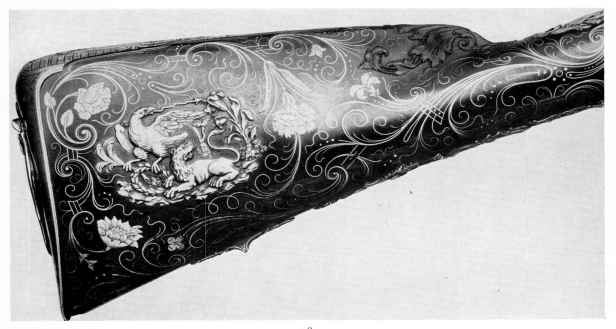

78

PLATE XXXIII: 72, sheet from French pattern book of 1749; 78, detail of air-gun on PLATE XXXI.

PLATE XXXIV: Pair of English double-barrelled flint-lock pocket pistols, dated 1823.